BOOK
OF
MAGIC

RITUAL BOOK OF MAGIC

CLIFFORD BIAS

SAMUEL WEISER, INC.

York Beach, Maine

First published in 1981 by
Samuel Weiser, Inc.
Box 612
York Beach, Maine 03910-0612

99 98 97 96 95 94
12 11 10 9 8 7 6 5

ISBN 0-87728-532-2
MG

Cover illustration is a painting titled "The Water Cup." Used by
kind permission of the artist.

Printed in the United States of America

The paper used in this publication meets the minimum require-
ments of the American National Standard for Permanence of Paper
for Printed Library Materials Z39.48-1984.

Do what thou wilt shall be the whole of the law;
for love is the law, love under will.

Contents

THE PYRAMID OF MAGIC

The Magus, the Theurgist, the True Witch stands on a pyramid of **power** whose foundation is **a profound knowledge of the occult,** whose four sides are **a creative imagination, a will of steel, a living faith** and **the ability to keep silent,** and whose internal structure is **love.**

For the purpose of securing your foundation:

1. Read and study **everything** of an Occult, Esoteric and Metaphysical nature that comes your way, **until** it dawns upon you that even in your reading and study you must exercise the first virtue of the Path of Attainment which is **discrimination.** Then begin more selective reading and study of such authors as Alice Bailey, Franz Bardon, Helena Blavatsky, W. E. Butler, Joseph Campbell, Aleister Crowley, Dion Fortune, Wm. G. Gray, G. I. Gurdjieff, Manly Palmer Hall, Max Heindel, Carl Jung, Gareth Knight, S. L. MacGregor Mathers, P. D. Ouspensky, Israel Regardie and Rudolph Steiner. One of the rules of many magical fraternities is "Read the ancient books of wisdom and try to understand their secret meaning." So purchase, read, study, meditate on and memorize large portions of the Holy Bible, the Koran, the Bhagavad-Gita and the Upanishads. To capture the "feel," the wonder and mystery of Magic, read Burton's unexpurgated translation of "The Arabian Nights," the English version by A. E. Watts of "The Metamorphoses of Ovid," Margaret Hunt's translation of "Fairy Tales" by the Brothers Grimm, and "The Song of Hiawatha" by Henry W. Longfellow.

2. Attain a practical working knowledge of Astrology and Tarot to the point of becoming proficient, even expert, in their use. Do the same with one or more other techniques of divination such as the I Ching (yee-jing), Numerology, Hand Analysis or Geomancy.

3. Follow the advice of the Masters to seek wisdom from nature. "Go to the ant, thou sluggard, consider her ways and be wise." Seek communion with nature by leisurely sojourns or trips into (not just through) the countryside—mountain, seashore, lake, stream, field, forest, woodland, farm, desert, city park—whatever is available—at different seasons and for varying lengths of time, the longer the better. If at all possible, have a garden of your own. Even in a city apartment it is possible to have at least one growing plant.

4. Seek to **know thyself,** perhaps by undergoing analysis by a competent psychoanalyst, having an Astrological Natal Chart erected and delineated by an expert Astrologer, or some other form of help from another person, but definitely and surely by getting into the habit of remembering and recording your dreams and by a **life-long habit of a daily period of meditation** lasting from a few minutes to several hours.

The very fact that you are reading this proves that you are imaginative. Feed and nurture your imagination. At first encourage it to become fervid, wild, uncontrolled. Then begin controlling it, make it do what you want, what you **will** it to do. For instance, without physical stimulus or cause, try to imagine to the point of a definite sensory response:

SEEING: (1.) an upright red equilateral triangle, (2.) the face of someone you love, (3.) an elf, (4.) a rainbow, (5.) yourself as a tiny infant, (6.) a flying horse, (7.) a cruxifixion;

HEARING   (1.) far-away church bells ringing, (2.) the voice of someone you love, (3.) furtive rustling, (4.) a woman sobbing, (5.) excited barking of dogs, (6.) a sexless mechanical voice speaking in a monotone, (7.) a violin playing "Home, Sweet Home";

SMELLING (1.) vanilla, (2.) a cesspool, (3.) new mown grass, (4.) decaying human flesh, (5.) summer rain, (6.) blood, (7.) newly baked bread;

TASTING   (1.) honey, (2.) salted peanuts, (3.) rancid meat, (4.) strawberries, (5.) a sour pickle, (6.) the bitterness of gall, (7.) ambrosia;

FEELING   (1.) a baby's toes, (2.) clammy cold, (3.) a tender kiss on your forehead, (4.) the strong handclasp of a good friend, (5.) a knife driven into your back, (6.) a woman's breast or a man's genitals, (7.) wind in your face.

Are you a weak-willed individual? **Make your will strong.** Are you a strong-willed person? **Make your will stronger.** The will is strengthened by being conscious of it, being aware of it, watching it, exercising it, seeking constantly to make it more definite, incisive, and firm. Do you never, seldom, often, usually, always keep your word? How about those "If you do so-and-so, I'll spank you!" type of threats or those "If you'll be good, I'll give you a treat!" types of promises to your children or more grown-up versions of such threats or promises to your family and friends? Do you keep appointments? How about those casually-made or just-to-be-polite promises to call or visit someone? **Resolve:** Beginning this very moment whatever I say I am going to do, **that I will do!** Come hell or high water **I will keep my word!** But also beginning this very moment **I will never make a promise that I do not intend to keep!** Moreover, I'll be most cautious and careful in giving my word or making a promise or a threat, for what I say I will do, **that I will do!**

How dependent are you on drugs, including pep pills, tranquilizers, aspirin, laxatives? How dependent are you on alcohol, tobacco, coffee, tea, soft drinks? Do you overeat? Is your physical body your master or your servant? Does it tell you what to do or do you tell it what to do? **Resolve: I will be the ruler of mine own domain!**

Do you have the ability to command? Is what you order or suggest usually obeyed or done? Do you give to others an appearance of poised and assured self-confidence, even of authority? Do you look others in the eye when you are talking to them? Do you enunciate clearly? Is your voice high or low pitched? **Challenge:** Without ostentation or arrogance, **I assume the air of authority.**

Can you **turn on** or **turn off** at will? Practice **total absorption** or **complete concentration** in or upon a particular situation, person or thing. At first choose those activities, people or things which are easy for you to give your complete attention to **so as to establish the habit of success,** then gradually move to those which require more and more **effort** of will to become totally absorbed in. Also practice **total indifference** or **complete unresponse,** again first choosing those activities, things and people to which it is easy for

2

you to be unresponsive, then moving on to those which are usually distracting and irritating. **Challenge: I can turn on or turn off at will.**

Your faith is what you really believe. Foster and strengthen your faith by using it, exercising it, enjoying it, depending upon it. To be alive is to respond to stimuli, to adapt, to change, to grow, to take in nutriment and to give off waste. Expect this of your faith, for what you want and must have is **a living faith.** And do not expect it to be reasonable and logical, scientific and pigeon-holed, for by its very nature it goes beyond so-called common sense, beyond everyday sense perception, beyond cerebral thinking, beyond reason and logic to "the substance of things hoped for, the evidence of things not seen."

There is much more to "the ability to keep silent" than the mere surface meaning, even though it means exactly that too! The real witch is neither the rattle-brained show-off chatterbox who titters archly, "I'm a witch, you know, tee hee, I'm going to put a charm on you, tee hee," nor the wrinkled stringy-haired harridan croaking, "Boil, boil, toil and trouble" to make some farmer's cows go dry, but a poised woman who can charm without saying a word. The real magus has neither the compulsion to parade in full magical regalia before the uninitiated, ranting pontifically on "Cosmic Consciousness," nor the need to buttonhole people at parties muttering darkly about attending a Black Mass. The deeper meaning of the quotation is the ability to become utterly still and silent, physically, emotionally, mentally, and thus to "Enter the Silence"—the doorway to the "Immeasurable Regions."

Love is the joy of becoming one with, of uniting with, of caring for and caring about, of giving to and receiving from, of affection and concern for —its source and parent and child, its partner and brother, its friend and mate—**Life.** And **love** is the internal structure of your Pyramid of Magic. So mote it be!

PROOF OF THE PUDDING

When the Moon is New, dance in a clockwise circle out-of-doors, saying or singing:

> Uranus, Diana and Mercury!
> Is Magic true? Can Magic be?
> A Magic Sign I'd have from thee—
> Shaddai El Chai and Ea, Ge!
> (shod-DOY el hoy, ee-uh, ge has a hard g.)
> A Magic Sign vouchsafe thou me.

After the sign appears, at Full Moon throw white or pale flowers into a brook, river, pool, pond, lake or ocean, saying or singing:

> Uranus, Diana and Mercury!
> A Magic Sign I asked of thee—
> A Magic Sign thou gav'st me,
> My thanks to thee, thrice blessd' be!
> Shaddai El Chai and Ea, Ge!

3

PRIVATE TEMPLE RITE

To be performed daily except when other Rites or Rituals take precedence and except during the dark of the Moon which is the seven-day period immediately before the New Moon.

Opening Exercises

Preliminary: Altar is a square table, such as a folding card table, covered with a black cloth. It is to be placed in the exact center of the room. On Altar is a white candle in a candlestick or holder in the south, a stemmed goblet with water in the west, a small dish of salt in the north, and a fan or a single fresh rose in a vase in the east. A side table such as an end table with a book of matches or a cigarette lighter and an ashtray is against the south wall of room. One straight chair in west facing east with small stand or end table at its left. On this stand is the Ritual Book.

You may be "sky-clad" (naked) or wearing a hooded long black robe which reaches from neck to ankles and has full open sleeves; sandals, no undergarments or hose. No money, no watch, no jewelry except wedding ring is to be carried or worn. Later, after magic insignia including girdle and pendant are consecrated, they may and should be worn. Always bathe prior to Temple Rite, if at all possible just immediately before.

If possible, enter Temple from the north or the west. Upon entering, salute the Altar by raising right arm, hand of which is a fist with thumb between forefinger and middle finger, to an angle of forty-five degrees, left hand flat on left breast. Then, hands returned to side, take three steps forward, stop, bow low from the waist, straighten, go to Altar and ignite candle, saying:

> From fire above to fire below,
> From fire within to fire without,
> May Michael's spear from there to here
> Make the magic fire appear.
> Above, below, within, without—
> Appear, fire appear!

Circumambulate deosil (clockwise, turning to the right) the Altar, saying:
> Round and round about this Temple I draw a magic circle, a magic circle of light!

Make one complete circuit of the Altar. Stop at chair, face Altar. Beginning with right arm stretched straight upward, forefinger extended, other fingers clasped to palm by thumb, draw a clock with sweeping motion of arm from up to right to down to left to up, saying:
> Round and round about this Temple I draw a magic circle, a magic circle of light!

Then draw another circle from down to front to up to back to down, saying:
> Round and round about this Temple I draw a magic circle, a magic circle of light!

Then say:
> Three magic circles have I drawn, that of space, that of time, and that of events. Without are other worlds, but this is mine. This is mine! I am its creator. I am its ruler. And so mote it be.

Sit. Facing east, spine straight, both feet flat on the floor and slightly

4

apart, hands resting palm down on thighs or knees, chin up, repeat aloud many, many times:

All the power that ever was, all the power that ever will be, is here right now.

Say it several times slowly, softly but distinctly. Then begin saying it louder and more rapidly, gradually increasing the volume and tempo until you are shouting it excitedly at great speed.

When you feel power surging within and around you, say:

Power is available to me by the simple act of my acceptance. I accept. I accept. I accept.

Take several deep breaths, inhaling through the nose, holding the breath a little longer than usual, exhaling audibly through the open mouth.

Now stand, raise both arms in adoration, head thrown back, and intone three times:

IAO! IAO! IAO! (Lips bared, jaws slightly apart, deepen or lower voice, saying: "Eeeeee!"
Throat and mouth wide open, say: "Ahhhhhh!"
Purse mouth in open circle, saying: "Ohhhhhh!")

Lower left arm to side. Perform the Quabalistic Cross: with thumb, forefinger and middle finger of right hand touch the center of the forehead between the eyebrows and say: "Thine." Touch the middle of the chest, saying: "Is the kingdom." Touch the right shoulder, saying: "And the power." Touch left shoulder, saying "And the glory." Hands together, open palms touching, extended fingers together, pointing upward as in prayer, bow head and say: "Forever and ever. Amen."

Immediately give the Sign of the Enterer: hands still together in the attitude of prayer, head still bowed, bend or bow slightly at the waist while advancing left foot forward a step. Short pause, maintaining pose. Then hands returned to side, straighten, feet together. Sit.

Enter the Silence, saying:

In the Name of the Lord of the Universe who works in silence and whom naught but the silence can express, I enter the silence.

Do so for at least two minutes, becoming absolutely quiet, utterly still.

Closing Exercises

Seated in the west, perform the Quabalistic Cross. Then, head still bowed and hands still together, intone HUA three times as Hoooooo-Ahhhhhh! On final intonation stand, raising head and at the same time shoving the hands upward over head, then outward and downward as a diver coming up out of water, letting the "ah" of the final HUA become an explosion or a bark with sharp expulsion of breath.

Immediately give the Sign of Silence: Press right forefinger firmly against closed lips, while mentally saying:

To will, to know, to dare, and to keep silent.
Love is the law, love under will.

Silently circumambulate widdershins (counter-clockwise, turning to the left) three times, stopping in the west. Bow, extinguish candle, take three steps backward, salute Altar as in Opening Exercises. The Rite is finished. Put things away, return room to its usual order, change to usual clothing. Blessed be!

5

Note: After the Magical Instruments, Weapons or Tools are acquired and consecrated, the Rod is placed on the Altar in the south, the Cup in the west, the Dagger in the east and the Disk in the north. After acquiring the Thurible or Censer, charcoal tablets and incense, ignite the charcoal after (or instead of) lighting the candle and cast the incense upon the glowing charcoal after the Sign of the Enterer.

STATIONS OF THE CIRCLED CROSS

Perform Opening Exercises of Temple Rite.

Seated in the west, read aloud:

The Circled Cross is one of the many emblems of Magic and the particular emblem of the Ancient Mystical Order of Seekers. It signifies the balance of all things in eternity and thus means equilibrium. The entire secret of the occult lies in the knowledge of equilibrium. Its attainment brings the greatest good, true wisdom and perfect happiness, because it brings realization of and at-one-ment with the One before whom no thing exists, the Single Source of Light, Love, Life and Law, the Lord of the Universe whose nature is One but whose manifestations are many, both male and female. This achievement of perfect equilibrium we call the Great Work and this I seek, now and forever.

Stand. Circumambulate deosil to south, face Altar and say:

In the SOUTH I stand. The element is FIRE. The letter of Tetragrammaton is YOD (yode). The God-Name is EL (el). The Archangel is MICHAEL (MICK-ah-el). The Angel is ARAL (ah-RAHL). The Principle is LIGHT. The season is SUMMER and the time is NOON. The gender is MASCULINE. Here force is POSITIVE, ACTIVE, ELECTRIC in nature.

With forefinger of right hand make a Circled Cross (up to down, right to left, then a circle clockwise beginning at the left) before the candle, saying:

I activate the fiery part of me and dedicate it to the performance of the Great Work.

Go to west, face Altar and say:

In the WEST I stand. The element is WATER. The letter of Tetragrammaton is HE (heh). The God-Name is ELOHIM (ELL-oh-keem). The Archangel is GABRIEL (GAH-bree-el). The Angel is TALIAHAD (tahl-ee-AH-had). The principle is LOVE. The season is AUTUMN and the time is DUSK. The gender is FEMININE. Here force is NEGATIVE, PASSIVE, MAGNETIC in nature.

With third or ring finger make Circled Cross before or over the goblet and say:

I activate the watery part of me and dedicate it to the performance of the Great Work.

Continue past north to east. Face Altar and say:

In the EAST I stand. The element is AIR. The letter of Tetragrammaton is VAU (vahv). The God-Name is the Tetragrammaton YAHWEH. The Archangel is RAPHAEL ((RAH-fah-el). The Angel is CHASSAN (hahs-SAN). The principle is LIFE. The season is SPRING and the time is DAWN. The gender is MASCULINE. Here also force is POSITIVE, ACTIVE, ELECTRIC in nature.

6

With little finger make Circled Cross before or over the rose or fan and say:

I activate the airy part of me and dedicate it to the performance of the Great Work.

Circumambulate deosil to north, face Altar and say:

In the NORTH I stand. The element is EARTH. The letter of Tetragrammaton is the final HE. The God-Name is ADONAI HA ARETZ (ah-doh-NOH-ee hah ah-RETZ). The archangel is AURIEL (AH-reeel). the Angel is PHORLAKH (fore-lock). The principle is LAW. The season is WINTER and the time is MIDNIGHT. The gender is FEMININE. Here also force is NEGATIVE, PASSIVE, MAGNETIC in nature.

With middle finger make Circled Cross over the salt, saying:

I activate the earthy part of me and dedicate it to the performance of the Great Work.

Continue deosil circumambulation while saying:

But through and beyond all directions I seek the CENTER. Using the four elements, I seek their source, the QUINTESSENCE. To this end (with thumb make Circled Cross on forehead) I activate my spiritual self and may it be dedicated to the performance of the Great Work

Finish circumambulation in the west. Sit. Again enter the Silence.

Perform Closing Exercise of Temple Rite.

Note: The ritual pronumciation of certain names is different from the usual. For instance, Michael is usually pronounced MIKE-el, but ritually it is MICK-ah-el, Elohim is usually pronounced el-OH-heem but in the liturgies it is said EL-oh-keem with a K sound on the last syllable instead of the usual H sound.

THE BINDING OF THE GIRDLE

Preliminary: When the Moon is waxing (going from New to Full), take three lengths of heavy gold, red or black cord or ribbon, the length exactly your own height, and braid them together, making a loop at one end and a tasseled knot at the other. This is your Magical Girdle which you are henceforth to wear whenever you perform a Rite of Magic. When the Moon is near or at Full, place the Girdle in the center of the Altar and

Perform Opening Exercises of Temple Rite.

Stand, approach Altar, go deosil to east. Take three pinches of salt from container in north and cast them (1) from up to down, (2) from right to left, (3) in clockwise circle beginning at left, into the goblet of water. Take up goblet into both hands, breathe onto the surface of water these words:

Water and Earth, where you are cast
Let no spell or purpose last
That's not in full accord with me!
For as my word, so mote it be.

With fingers of left hand sprinkle a few drops of the salted water on the Girdle, saying:

Made to measure,
Wrought to bind—

Blessed be
This cord entwined.

Cup hands around candle flame, bend over and whisper to the flame:

Creature of fire, this charge I lay—
No evil in thy presence stay!
Hear my word addressed to thee—
And as my word, so mote it be.

Without singeing it, pass the Girdle across the candle flame, saying:

Made to measure,
Wrought to bind—
Blessed be
This cord entwined.

Put Girdle around waist, tying it and letting the ends hang down in front as you say:

As I am bound so can I bind
Things and creatures of any kind.
"Do what thou wilt!" was said to me,
And as I will, so mote it be.

Loosen the Girdle, letting it fall to the floor as you say:

As I am free so can I free
Things and creatures bound by me.
For love is the law, so says the lore
Of light and life for evermore.

Take Girdle and hold high its looped end, saying:

Ever it is the duty of the brother above
To stoop to help the brother below.
EVOHE! EVOHE! EVOHE! (aah-voh-aiee)
Ye Great Ones beyond and behind our being!
Ye Old Ones out of the Night of Time!
You Masters and Adepts who have attained!
This is my measure, this Cable Tow.
Take it and pull me, lift me, lead me up to where you are, for where
you are, there would I be!

Hold tasseled end down as if to those below you and say:

Ever it is the duty of the brother above to stoop to help the brother
below.
Harken, my brothers and sisters, human, elemental, animal, vegetable, mineral!
All you who are below me in the scale of evolution, I offer you my
aid!
Take the Cable Tow and strive with me, for where I am there shall
you be!

Retie Girdle about your waist, saying:

As I am bound so am I free.
As I give help so it comes to me.
Such is the law and so mote it be.

Return deosil to seat in west. Sit.

Perform Closing Exercises of Temple Rite.

8

GIRDLE MAGIC

Much magical work can be done with the Girdle. For that which is here given you will need, in addition to your consecrated girdle, an "object link".

Object Links

Links with the person on whom the magical effect is being worked are, in the order of their potency:
1. A drop of his semen if a male or a drop of her menstrual blood if a female,
2. a drop of his or her blood,
3. hair or nail clippings of the person,
4. a piece of clothing that has been worn by the person, the more intimately the better,
5. his or her signature,
6. his or her photograph or
7. the Tarot Court Card most nearly representative,
8. The person's full name written on virgin parchment in the blood of the one who desires the effect,
9. his or her name written on white paper with red ink or pencil by one who desires the effect, or
10. the same written by you.

The lesser the potency of the object-link, the greater must be your concentrated will power.

Impersonal object-links are:
1. A symbol such as the Tarot Ten of Pentacles to represent prosperity,
2. a picture representing the desired effect,
3. the desired effect or result clearly (both in meaning and legibility) and briefly written, on virgin parchment in blood or
4. on white paper with red ink or pencil.

The Voice of Experience

Never attempt a magical working that deep within yourself you are convinced is impossible, for such will surely be a failure. Never attempt a magical working that goes contrary or is diametrically opposed to your basic nature or character. that "goes against the grain", for such will surely be a failure. Remember the admonition, "You must believe in your own magic or it won't work!" Remember also the aphorism, "In order to get results on any plane of existence, energy belonging or converted to that plane must be expended." So, needless to say, GREAT EMOTION and WILL POWER are essential components of any magical practice and must be expressed to the point of feeling utterly exhausted for a time afterward. Get into the HABIT OF SUCCESS by working the simpler effects first. It is wise to perform a divination concerning the affair before working. If the divination is unfavorable, do not attempt the magic practice. And note that the results frequently are seemingly by co-incidence or happenstance.

Snaring or Capturing

To snare the attention and interest of someone who could be of help in furthering your career, of a prospective employer, of a possible good friend or lover, etc. On the New Moon or within seven days thereafter, upon the Altar put your girdle with tasseled end threaded through the looped end so as to make of it a snare or lasso, arranging it in a circle. On center of Altar, inside the circle of the girdle, put the object-link. If you know the person, use a personal object-link. If it is to be someone whom you as yet do not know, use an impersonal object-link such as the Magician of the Tarot for "a clever man". Also on Altar but outside the circle of the girdle are candle or Rod, goblet or Cup with red wine, rose, fan or Dagger, and salt or Disk.

Perform Opening Exercises of Temple Rite. Approach Altar from the west, take goblet or Cup, hold it high and say:

> In the west I stand, the station of the suppliant.
> By the virtures of the Cup I seek the aid of the Elder Ones.
> EVOHE! EVOHE! EVOHE!
> Ye Great Ones beyond and behind my being!
> Ye Old Ones out of the Night of Time!
> Lend me thine aid!

Spill a little of the wine. Replace goblet or Cup. Circumambulate deosil to east, face Altar and say:

> In the east I stand, the station of the hierophant, the one who knows, the one who can!

Carefully and deliberately arrange girdle around the object-link, saying:

> This trap I set, this snare I lay
> To catch the eye of the one I say.
> (Call the name or the title of the person three times.)
> Your attention and interest are drawn to me—
> And as I will, so mote it be!

Draw the girdle slowly around the object-link, singing:

> Te dum, te dum, te tittle de dum—
> You go along unwary—
> But here I catch you in my snare—
> YOU are my quarry.

Tighten the girdle. Pause in exultation. Go deosil to west, sit, perform Closing Exercises of Temple Rite, omitting the widdershins circumambulation. If possible leave the object-link within the girdle on the Altar for three days.

For an increase in finances, a job, to capture a contract, sale, etc., use an impersonal object-link and substitute the following:

> This trap I set, this snare I lay
> To catch the essence of what I say.
> (Name it three times.)
> Its body and substance will come to me—
> And as I will, so mote it be!

Binding

Waxing Moon. Object-link on center of Altar surrounded by the symbols of the elements. The girdle is worn. Opening Exercises of Temple Rite. Approach Altar from west, same action and words as above for "In the west I stand, etc." and "In the east I stand, etc." Then tighten girdle about your waist, saying:

> As I am bound so can I bind
> Things and creatures of any kind.

10

"Do what thou wilt!" was said to me,
And as I will so mote it be!

Take object-link into both hands, fondle it, croon to it, make love to it. Then tuck it under robe against your solar-plexus, binding it there with girdle and say:

Together, together, are we to be—
For precious, precious, thou art to me,
And precious, precious, am I to thee!
I bind you (name).
I bind you (name).
I bind you (name).
Your very being is bound to me—
Thou to me and I to thee!
And as I will so mote it be!

Be very careful to bind the object-link securely against your person, for if it falls the spell is broken. Exult, go deosil to west, sit, perform Closing Exercises omitting the widdershins circumambulation. If possible, wear the object-link on your body for three days.

Loosening

To loosen so as to be free of the hold on you of another person or of your own hold upon another, an unwanted habit (smoking, drinking, etc.), an onerous task, a negative thought form, etc. Waxing Moon. Have a broom and dust pan in the north. When dressing for the Rite, put the object-link next to your skin, binding it there with the girdle. Opening Exercises of Temple Rite. Approach Altar from the west, same action and words as above for "In the west I stand, etc." and "In the east I stand, etc."

Slowly and deliberately loosen the girdle, allowing the object-link to fall to the floor, while saying:

What is bound by me I can set free;
Such is the law and so mote it be!
I can set free what is bound to me;
Such is my will and so mote it be!

With forefinger of right hand (or with Rod) make widdershins (counter-clockwise) circle three times around object-link, saying:

No more together are we to be bound.
No longer together are we to be found.
(Name it three times.)
You go your way and I'll go mine,
And never, no never will we entwine.
(Name it three times.)
Forever and ever you're rid of me,
Forever and ever I'm rid of thee.
(Name it three times.)
May fate and fortune take you away,
For parted are we, beginning this day!

With broom, sweep the object-link into the dust pan. Carry it thus three time widdershins around the Altar and take it outside door or outside the

11

circle via the north. Return and perform the Closing Exercises of Temple Rite. Do not pick up the object-link with your bare hands, use paper as insulation. If possible, throw object-link into running water or flush it down the toilet, saying:

Hekas! Hekas! Este bibeloi!
(Hay-kahs Hay-kahs ESS-tay be-bay-LOH-ee)
Be far from me, so mote it be!

THE ADVENTURE OF THE MAGICAL ROD

Purchase a new and very sharp hatchet or hand-axe, without haggling. Explain to no one what you want it for. Wash it thoroughly with soap in warm water, saying:

Be clean, good hatchet (axe), be clean of all contamination. Hekas! Hekas! Este Bibeloi! Be far from here, O ye profane! I wash all adverse conditions from this instrument, that it may be pure to do the work I intend it to do. Be clean, good hatchet (axe), be clean.

Rinse and dry it, lovingly. Touch the cutting edge lightly, saying:

Be sharp, good hatchet (axe), be sharp.

May you do your work well.

Wrap it in clean paper or cloth and put it in a safe place where no one will handle or touch it until you intend to use it.

Choose a "special place" where Hazel, Ash, Poplar, Flowering Almond, Cedar or Oak trees are growing. Be able to identify the species of tree. Secure permission to cut a branch. A living tree that has survived being struck by lightning is perfect.

Choose a "special day" and perhaps even a "special time" that has significance to you. Your birthday, a Sunday, day of the New Moon or Full Moon, or Moon in Leo. Anytime from midnight to noon. Not in the dark of the Moon.

Taking your consecrated hatchet or axe, a burlap or cloth bag or wrapping for the tree branch, and a "libation" or a gift for the tree from which the branch will come, go, alone if at all possible, to the special place on the special day and cut, with one stroke, a special straight branch about three feet long and not thicker than your thumb and not smaller than your little finger, from the special tree. The branch you cut must not, and should never, touch the ground. Make a libation by pouring a little water at the foot of the tree or give the tree a gift such as some fertilizer or manure, saying something such as: "Thank you, brother tree, for the branch which will become my Magical Rod! Here's a little token of my appreciation. Use it in good health!" Trim the branch of excess length and any twigs or leaves, wrap it in the burlap or cloth, and take it home. Show it to no one, allow no one but yourself to touch it. Practice a little deception if you must by cutting a second branch to show to curious family or friends who know of your expedition, later discarding the second branch. The hatchet or hand-axe has now fulfilled its purpose, and it may be put in your tool chest.

When the Moon is approaching the Full and in your own Sun Sign or Rising Sign or in a Fire Sign, make and consecrate your Magical Rod. You will need for this a very sharp pocket knife or paring knife, a stemmed goblet of water, a white candle, a rose in a vase, a gold coin if possible, otherwise a shiny penny. In addition, two pill boxes, marked plus for male and minus for female, containing cotton. The cotton of the plus box should have a drop or two of the semen of a virile young human male, the cotton of the minus box a drop or two of the menstrual blood of a virgin young human female. If these two substances are completely impossible to obtain, then prick the right forefinger for a drop of blood for the plus box, prick the left forefinger for a drop of blood for the minus box. You will also need some coarse and fine sandpaper and a yard of silk or silk-like synthetic material, white, yellow, orange, red or black in color, as wrapping for the Magical Rod when not in use.

On Altar place the burlap-covered branch in the center, the goblet of water and the open minus pill box in the west, the candle and the open plus pill box in the south, the rose east, and the coin north. The sharp knife, sandpaper and covering for the Rod are at hand on a side table. Chair in west, facing east.

Sky-clad or robed, girded and sandaled, perform Opening Exercises of Temple Rite.

Move chair close to Altar. Sit. From east to south to west to north (the "direction of the winds") move the goblet of water, the candle, the rose and the coin to the corners of the Altar, saying:

> Take your stations, Symbols of the Elements. Guard well this Temple where a Magic Rite is being performed.

Move the minus pill box in the same direction to the north. Thus you are sitting in the west, facing east, with a cleared space before you. Take the tree branch from its wrapping and, using the sharp knife and sandpaper, make a Magical Rod of it. Peel it carefully and cut away all protuberances. Its length should be either the length of your own spine or the length from elbow to end of longest finger. The smaller end should be gently rounded, not honed to a sharp point. This is the male end, the point. The other end, the base, should be flat, but notched like an arrow where the bow-string fits. This is the female end. The whole thing should be as beautiful as you can make it, straight and round and smooth. The important thing is, make it yourself, unassisted. Wrap the debris in the burlap and put it aside. Place the Rod on the Altar, pointing east.

Stand. Raise both arms in adoration and say:

> Holy art Thou, Lord of the Universe!
> Holy art Thou, whom nature hath not formed.
> Holy art Thou, the vast and the mighty One.
> Lord of the light and of the darkness.

Arms returned to sides, circumambulate deosil the Altar. Stop in south, face Altar, spread hands over Rod and say:

> El! El! El!
> Michael! Michael! Michael!
> Aral! Aral! Aral!

Pick up the Rod. Touch its male end lightly to the candle flame, saying:
> And thou who art president over fire of Fire!

Touch the female end lightly to the water, saying:
> And thou who art president over fluid Fire!

Touch the male end to the rose and say:
> And thou who art president over subtle and aspiring Fire!

13

Touch female end to coin and say:

> And thou who art president over the denser aspects of Fire!

Hold the Rod, male end upward, with both hands, right hand above, left hand below, thumbs pointing up along line of Rod, and say:

> Endow this Rod with hidden forces and occult virtues so that I may be enabled with it to perform aright those magical operations for which I now dedicate it. I dedicate you, Rod, to the performances of true Magic! (Touch the female end to the cotton in the minus box.) Be thou fertile! (Touch the male end to the cotton in the plus box.) Be thou potent!

Holding Rod in both hands, walk slowly from south to west. Stop in west, place Rod on Altar, sit. Enter the Silence. Perform Closing Exercises of Temple Rite. Wrap the Rod in its cloth and put it in a safe place. The two pill boxes, along with the debris and the burlap, must be burned.

ROD MAGIC

The ROD, the SCEPTRE or the WAND is the first of the four INSTRU-MENTS, TOOLS or WEAPONS of Magic and is associated with the Yod of Tetragrammaton and the Element of Fire. It represents the WILL of the Magus or Theurgist, his WISDOM, his WORD, his LIGHT, his SPIRIT.

The Magic Barrier

To prevent intruders entering your house.

When the Moon is waxing and in a Fire Sign or in your own Sun Sign or Rising Sign, perform Opening Exercises of Temple Rite.

Seated in the west, read:

> It is my will to protect this house (apartment) from intruders. It is my will that no one may enter this house (apartment) without authority or right to do so. It is my will that no one may enter this house (apartment) without permission or invitation. "Do what thou wilt" was said to me; and as I will so mote it be!

Arise, go deosil to south. Take Rod and hold it male end upward in the right hand, thumb pointing up along line of Rod. Say:

> This consecrated Rod is the instrument of my will. It is a Sceptre of Power. It is the Wand of the Magus of the Eternal. (Elevate Rod.) By the Power of Yah and the Yod of Tetragrammaton, may this house (apartment) be protected from all intruders! ELOHIM GE-BOR! (EL-oh-keem. G is hard . . . ge-BORE.)

Lower Rod but still hold it upright in right hand. Holding it thus, go to every door, window, or opening of the house or apartment. At each, hold the Rod horizontally, thumbs toward the center and tips touching, male end right, female end left. Thus you create a bar across each opening. Say at each:

> Without authority you may not enter! Without the right, you may not enter! Without invitation you may not enter! Such is my will and so mote it be!

14

Return to Temple, circumambulate deosil to south, return Rod to Altar, go to the west, sit, enter the Silence, perform Closing Exercises of Temple Rite.

Dissolving a Barrier

With left hand hold the Rod's female end in contact with your solar plexus, the left thumb pointing toward the male end of the Rod. With right hand grip the middle of the Rod with thumb pointing toward the male end. Thus the Rod is pointing straight out in front of you. Visualize the barrier before you. Vividly imagine and will a stream of force shooting forth from the male end of the Rod, like a flame-thrower, dissolving the barrier. Name the barrier three times and say:

Open! In the Name of El!
or
With the fiery force of Michael I dissolve you!

Magic Welcoming

With Rod in hand stand just inside the door to your Temple or home. Visualize some desirable, loved or welcome visitor standing or being just outside the door. This may be a person, an other-world entity, or a wanted or needed thing. With left hand, palm down and thumb extending along line of Rod, grasp female end of Rod and hold it to the left side of doorway. With right hand, palm up and thumb pointing also toward male end of Rod, hold Rod to the right side of doorway. Then with right hand draw the male end of the Rod toward you, stepping back as if opening a door, name the visitor three times and say:

Welcome! Welcome! Welcome! Enter in Peace!

CHANNEL OF SCINTILLATING FLAME

An incense burner in the form of a swinging censer or thurible such as those used in Roman Catholic or Eastern Orthodox churches is now to be acquired and consecrated. Frankincense (also called Olibanum) and charcoal tablets are to be provided.

Moon approaching the Full and in a Fire Sign.

Censer with charcoal and container of Frankincense are with lighter swings forward. Replace Censer. Continue circumambulation deosil to north. are Rod in south, goblet of water in west, coin or dish or salt in north, and rose or fan in east. One chair in the west, another in the north.

Perform Opening Exercises of Temple Rite, igniting the charcoal at the time and instead of lighting the candle.

Seated in the west, read:

Fire is the only Element that cannot be directly handled either physically or on other planes without causing damage. It is dangerous. Yet it has been man's control of fire that has brought him civilization, and without it life itself does not exist. In Magic, fire must be understood as signifying light and illumination in all possible meanings and on all possible levels. It also signifies the fire of creativity in all possible meanings and on all possible levels. Just as nature supplies the materials that in proper grouping and with application of proper force we can make fire, just as nature supplies the sexual equipment, substances and drive that in proper grouping and with proper stimulation and opportunity we can create offspring, so does nature on all levels of existence supply the materials for illumination and creation to take place. Michael awaits to stretch forth his spear and allow fire to transfer from one level to another. Abednego was the name of one of the three Hebrews in Daniel's story of the fiery furnace. The name means "servant of the shining fire." The Theurgist becomes a servant of the shining fire when he assembles nature's materials in proper grouping and opens the gateway for Michael to do his work.

Stand. Circumambulate deosil to south. Stop in south, remove cover of Censer, take handful of Frankincense and cast it onto the glowing charcoal, replace cover. Take Rod from Altar and with it make Circled Cross over Censer, saying:

In honor of Michael, "who is like God," Prince of Heaven, Archangel of Fire, Regent of the South, Angel of Purification, Captain of the Angelic Army, I consecrate this Censer to the burning of incense in the Rites of Magic.

Replace Rod on Altar. Take Censer by the swinging chains and cense the Altar with three swings to the left, three swings to the right, and three swings forward. Replace Censer. Continue circumambulation deosil to north. Sit in north, facing south. Read aloud:

An open gateway in the heaven with stars above and below. Beyond the gate is Light, ineffable Light. Standing in the gatway is a triumphant Angel with spear uplifted and shining face of courage. Upon the starry threshold is his name: Michael, Like Unto God.

Become utterly still for a moment. Then, in the south, vividly visualize a vast angelic figure, conceived of in the traditional conventional style, with uplifted spear. The form to be visualized will have a predominance of flaming red touched here and there with vivid flashes of emerald green. Little tongues of fire will lick the browned earth about the bare feet. Adore in silence for another long moment. A radiation of heat from the figure should be sensed. The emanation from the Archangel penetrates and purifies. Warmth at first of gentle degree, increasing in intensity until it burns and utterly consumes every blemish which troubles the personality. Finally say:

Mighty Michael whose name means "who is like God," thanks be to thee for thy purifying fire. I would be a channel of the scintillating flame. I would be a servant of the shining fire. Enflame thou me!

Stand. Raise both hands to forehead, palms outward, thumbs along line of eyebrows, tips touching. Tips of forefingers touching. Thus you make an upward pointing triangle on your forehead which is the Sign of Fire.

Hands returned to sides, circumambulate deosil to west. Sit. Perform Closing Exercises of Temple Rites. If possible have a record or tape of the Magic Fire Music of Wagner's "Die Walkure" playing during the rite.

Whenever there is a special need for courage, whenever great danger threatens, whenever a blemish or defect needs to be burned away, and on the Feast of Michael, September 29, with the same set-up as above perform the following:

1. Opening Exercises of Temple Rite.
2. Cense the Altar.
3. Circumbulate to north. Sit. Say:

> In time of need I turn to (On this his feast day I honor) Michael, "who is like God," Prince of Heaven, Archangel of Fire, Regent of the South, Angel of Purification, Captain of the Angelic Army.

4. Visualize Michael in the south. Adore in silence or whisper the need.
5. Stand. Make Sign of Fire. Say:

> Blessed be Michael, Like Unto God!

6. Return to west, sit.
7. Closing Exercises of Temple Rite.

THE HOLY GRAIL

Spend considerable time in choosing your Elemental Instrument of Water —the Cup. (Traditionally it is received as a gift from a loved one.) A Chalice such as those used in liturgical Christian churches for Holy Communion is most excellent. These usually are silver-plated with the inside of the cup gold-plated and can be ordered from church supply houses. However, a stemmed crystal or glass goblet is also appropriate. If crystal, it should be used as is, but if glass, eight flower petals should be painted on, colored with bright blue edged with bright orange. The Divine Name ELOHIM, the Archangelic Name GABRIEL, and the symbols of Cancer, Scorpio and Pisces should be drawn in bright orange. The Cup should be washed, dried and polished before it is consecrated and, if silver, have a draw-string cloth bag to keep it untarnished when not in use.

Moon approaching the Full and in a Water Sign.

On the Altar is the empty Cup in the center, Rod and candle in the south, a small pitcher of water in the west, a rose in a vase east, and a small dish of salt north. Censer with charcoal and lighter or matches on stand in the south. The incense is Myrrh. Chair in west, facing east.

Perform Opening Exercises of Temple Rite, igniting the charcoal at the time of lighting the candle.

Stand. Raise both arms in adoration. Say:

> Holy art thou, Lord of the Universe!
> Holy art thou, whom nature hath not formed.
> Holy art thou, the vast and the mighty One.
> Lord of the light and of the darkness!

Arms returned to side, circumambulate deosil to south, face Altar. Take Rod in right hand and make counter-clockwise circle over Cup, saying:

> By the power of Yah, the Yod of Tetragrammaton and the Wand of Will, I exorcise and free from any and all contamination this Cup. Hekas! Hekas! Este Bibeloi! Be far from here, O ye profane! I declare this Cup to be virgin!

17

Replace Rod. Turn to Censer, cast the incense upon the glowing charcoal and cense the Altar with three swings left, three swings right and three swings forward. Replace Censer. Go to west, face Altar, spread hands over Cup and say:

> Elohim! Elohim! Elohim!
> Gabriel! Gabriel! Gabriel!
> Taliahad! Taliahad! Taliahad!

Pick up the Cup in both hands. Hold it over the candle flame, saying:

> And thou who art ruler over the fiery Waters!

Hold it over the pitcher of water and say:

> And thou who art ruler over the pure and fluid Element of Water.

Hold it over the rose and say:

> And thou who art ruler of the etheric and airy qualities of Water.

Hold it over the dish of salt and say:

> And thou who art ruler of the more dense and solid qualities of Water.

Elevate the Cup with both arms stretched upward, saying:

> Endow this Cup with hidden forces and occult virtues so that I may be enabled with it to perform aright those magical operations for which I now dedicate it.

Lower the Cup to eye level and say:

> I dedicate you, Cup, to the performance of true Magic.

Kiss the Cup and say:

> Fount of Life, Vehicle of the Spirit, Womb of the Mother, Bringer-Forth of Form, I love you!

Place Cup on Altar and say:

> Great Mother! Matron of Many Names! Sakti, Tefnut, Cybele, Demeter, Rhea, Hera, Juno, Frigga, Isis, Soma, Kwan Yin, Habondia, Aradia! This is your Instrument. Bless it and me!

With third or ring finger make Circled Cross over Cup. Then pour water from pitcher into Cup, saying:

> Receive, consecrated Cup, your own element of Water!

Take Cup and drink the water after saying:

> I receive and am grateful for the love of the Mother!

Replace Cup. Sit. Enter the Silence. Perform Closing Exercises of Temple Rite.

CUP MAGIC

The CUP, or the CHALICE, is the second of the four instruments, tools or weapons of Magic and is associated with the first He of Tetragrammaton and the Element of Water. It represents the LOVE of the Magus or Theurgist, his UNDERSTANDING, his COMPASSION, his RECEPTIVITY, his SOUL.

Charging the Cup

In your kitchen sink or a large bowl of water, take a teacup and plunge it under the surface of the water. The teacup is thus full of water. Keeping it under the water, turn it upside down and move it around. Magically you have emptied the cup even though it is still full of water. Now lift it out of the water, emptying it of water as you do so, but see it filling with air which replaces the water as the content of the cup. Next, breathe into the cup filling it with your breath and thus emptying it of its air content. This is to help you realize that we only **change** the contents of a cup, that to fill it with one thing is to empty it of something else. You might even take an air-filled cup and pour in water, realizing that the displaced air is overflowing into the atmosphere to make room for the water. Then pour sand into the water-filled cup until it has displaced the water. Thus you have a change of content from gas to liquid to solid. Then reverse the process by washing out the sand and blowing out the water. Note that the contents of the cup depend on which element is active and which passive. The Cup is both a holder for the passive and an arena for the active elements either successively or simultaneously.

From the above we can see that the best way to describe the content of a Cup would be to speak of its "charge," and this is the correct magical term. The Cup is said to be in a state of "charge" with whatever is willed into it. Now experiment in charging your Cup. Fill it with light from the rays of Sun or Moon and then "drink" the light. Breathe into the Cup a bad habit, a state of depression, an illness, the name of an unwanted person or thing in your life; empty the Cup by turning it upside down and naming three times what you are getting rid of, adding:

Begone! Begone! Be far from me!
And as I will, so mote it be!

Afterward, charge the Cup with your love, saying:

Fount of Life, Vehicle of the Spirit, Womb of the Mother, Bringer Forth of Form, I love you!

while kissing the Cup. After EVERY magical use of the Cup, ALWAYS recharge it with your love.

Fill the Cup with water and then water potted plants with it as a ritual act, becoming a priest or priestess of the Great Mother in supplying the plants with life-giving water without which they would die. Assume the stance of the Water Bearer of Aquarius, fill the Cup with love and pour it out in blessing upon parched, dry earth.

Drinking and Toasting

Obtain a photograph of some loved person with whom contact is sought. Fill the Cup with some suitable drink. Arrange the photograph so that its image is reflected in the Cup when it is held correctly before the eyes (milk provides a fine reflecting surface). Concentrate on the reflected image, seeing it not as a photograph but as the individual in person in the Cup. Intone three times the person's name vibrantly across the surface of the fluid so that it ripples to the sound. The contents of the Cup are now charged with the name and likeness of the person. Magically, they are "in the Cup." Drink the contents of the Cup while holding a thought of love for the person, or mentally saying:

I take you to be a part of me; and as I will so mote it be!

We may do this with anyone we love, either human or divine, and so make them part of ourselves. In time, do away with the need of a photograph or physical reflection and visualize the being "live" in the Cup. Make them therein move, smile, respond. Sooner or later they will do something other than what you had intended to visualize them doing. This will be your Clairvoyance manifesting.

In toasting, the Cup is raised, the person or thing being honored is named, and the contents of the Cup is drunk. Often a wish or a kindly thought is expressed: "to your health," "good luck," "to the bride, God bless her," etc. In Magic, the toast usually is, "Do what thou wilt shall be the whole of the Law," to which the response is, "Love is the Law, Love under Will."

Libation and Lustration

To "make a libation" is to offer liquid refreshment to non-human or spiritual beings by outpouring from the Cup in a suitably symbolic manner. A libation is a greeting, a good-will offering, a proffer of friendship, a token of love, respect or gratitude. Whenever opportunity occurs, throw wine or an alcoholic drink into flames, saying, "I salute the Powers of Fire!" Pour water into pool, stream, lake or ocean, saying, "I salute the Powers of Water!" Fling water or wine to the winds, saying, "I salute the Powers of Air!" Pour water, beer, ale, wine upon the ground, saying, "I salute the Powers of the Earth!" Of course, other more personal salutations may be used and petitions made: "Ho, Michael! Protect me!" "Bless me, Great Mother!" "Blow, blow, brother Wind! May I ride the wind home." "Thank you, Mother Earth, for all your bounty!" etc.

To "lustrate" means to use moving water for cleansing and purification purposes. The simplest way of doing this is by taking a shower. When showering make mental and spiritual cleansing movements as well as physical ones by holding the thought of riding yourself of non-physical dirt along with the physical dirt. Remember that all dirt is only misplaced matter capable of being re-used elsewhere. The energy we tie up or confine in hatred, resentment, envy, fear, etc., can be used constructively elsewhere in our lives. When showering, say something such as, "I have been very resentful lately. I don't want this. It endangers my health on inner as well as outer levels. I want to be free of it, and, besides, its energy is needed elsewhere. Water, water, wash it away, and take it where it ought to go, down the drain." Washing the hands under a tap of running water while naming and willing away any undesirable influence is an excellent method of lustration.

Visualization and Clairvoyance

Visualization is "willed imagination," the ability to "image" or "see" mentally at will. Some people have this ability naturally, but in most it needs to be activated and cultivated. It is a prerequisite to Clairvoyance. Cup three-quarters full of water before you on Altar or table, sit, elbows on table, thumbs held between forefinger and middle finger of clenched hands, checkbones resting on "ball" or "heel" of hands, gazing into the water, practice visualization. At first, will yourself to see single, simple objects or symbols. Begin with a Silver Crescent, a symbol of Magic of Water. After you can see this clearly in the water before you, practice with the other "Tattwas," as they are called.

AKASA is Spirit or Aether, its symbol is a black or indigo egg or oval. TEJAS or AGNI is Fire, its symbol is an upright red equilateral triangle. APAS is Water, its symbol is a silver crescent. VAYU is Air, its symbol is a sky-blue circle or disc. PRITHIVI is Earth, its symbol is a yellow square or cube.

After you can visualize each one singly, try them in this combination:

AKASA of APAS, the most tenuous or spiritual aspect of Water, a small black egg on a larger silver crescent;

TEJAS of APAS, Fire of Water, as Rain, swift passionate attack, a small red triangle on a larger silver crescent;

VAYU of APAS, Air of Water, as ocean currents or waves, steady force, a small blue circle on a larger silver crescent;

PRITHIVI of APAS, Earth of Water, as ice, congealed force, a small yellow square on a larger silver crescent.

Holding the partly-filled Cup in both hands close to chest and with elbows pressed to the sides, sit where a gleam of light from a burning candle is reflected on the surface of the water. The tremors of your body will cause the reflected gleam to dance. Gazing steadily at this gleam, will the inner vision to unfold.

Outdoors when the Moon is Full have a friend or fellow Theurgist so hold a mirror that it catches the Moon and reflects it into your Cup where you have put a white or pink rose and covered it with white wine. Gazing into the Cup, say: "Mother, mother, mother, here's a rose for thee. Mother, mother, mother, what's in store for me?" Afterward pour the rose and wine into a stream or pool.

Crystal Ball or Magic Mirror

A Crystal Ball or a Magic Mirror (a concave tinted mirror) may now be purchased, if you like. Neither is a necessary tool or instrument of Magic. However, many Theurgists feel they need a crystal ball or magic mirror to "scry" with. "Scrying" is a term applied to crystal-gazing. If a ball or mirror is desired, it should be washed, dried and polished and then exorcised before it is consecrated.

Exorcism: With Rod make widdershins (counter-clockwise) circle over the object, saying:

By the power of Yah, the Yod of Tetragrammaton and the Wand of Will, I exercise and make clean of any and all contamination and negative influence this ball of crystal (mirror of magic). Hekas! Hekas! Este Bibeloi!

The consecration ceremony may be based upon or similar to that of the

Cup. The Act of Consecration: With ring or third finger make Circled Cross over object, saying:

> An object for scrying be thou to me, and as I will so mote it be!

MESSENGER OF HEAVEN

Moon waxing in a Water Sign.

On Altar are Rod in south, Cup with water in west, rose or fan in east, and coin or salt in north. Censer with charcoal and lighter or matches and container of incense on stand in south. The incense is Myrrh. One chair east, another west.

Perform Opening Exercises of Temple Rite igniting the charcoal at the time and instead of lighting the candle.

After entering the Silence while sitting in the west, stand, go deosil to south, cast incense upon the glowing charcoal and cense the Altar. Replace Censer, continue deosil to east. Sit in east, facing west. Read aloud:

> An open gateway in the heavens with stars above and below. Beyond the gate is silvery mist glowing from an unseen Moon. Through the gateway flows a stream of clearest water where a luminous Angel stands with bare feet awash. A tender smile upon his lips, he holds aloft with both hands the silver Grail Cup which glows with shining aura. In the water about his feet is his name: Gabriel, the Potent of God.

Become utterly still for a moment. Then, in the west, vividly visualize a vast Angelic figure conceived of in the traditional, conventional style, with uplifted Cup. The form to be visualized will have a predominance of blue, offset by orange. Adore in silence.

A radiation of potency from the figure should be sensed, causing a stirring in the heart and sexual organs. The emanation from the Archangel cleanses and purifies, dissolving impurities and superfluities, returning these back to earth for transmutation.

Stand. Take the Cup and elevate it high in both hands, saying:

> I honor Gabriel, "The Potent of God," Messenger of Heaven, Archangel of Water, Regent of the West, Life-bearer powered by Love, who helps Force turn into Form.

Drink the contents of the Cup. Re-charge it with love by kissing it and saying:

> Fount of Life, Vehicle of the Spirit, Womb of the Mother, Bringer-forth of Form, I love you!

Replace Cup. Make Sign of Water: Place both open hands downward flat against stomach or solar plexus, thumbs along line of diaphragm, tips touching. Fingers extended, tips of forefingers touching. Thus you make a downward pointing triangle. Say:

> Potent Gabriel! Thanks be to thee for thy cleansing and refreshing Water. Messenger of Heaven, thou art, thy messenger I would be!

Hands returned to side, circumambulate deosil to west, sit. Perform Closing Exercises of Temple Rite. If possible have a record or tape playing

music suggestive of water during the rite, such as Handel's "Water Music."
This ceremony should also be performed (a.) whenever there is a need for cleansing and purification, (b.) for potency in either or both its physical and spiritual aspects, and (c.) on March 24th, the Feast of Gabriel.

THE ELEMENTAL WEAPON OF AIR

Procure a steel dagger, the most beautiful and best shaped you can find. Haggle not over the price. Wash, rinse, dry and polish it.

Moon approaching the Full and in an Air Sign.

On Altar is the dagger in the center, Rod and candle in the south, Cup with water in the west, a rose in a vase east, small dish of salt north. Incense: Galbanum if possible, otherwise a mixture of equal parts of dried Rose Petals and Lavender.

Perform Opening Exercises of Temple Rite.

Stand, raise both arms in adoration and repeat the "Holy art thou" prayer. Arms returned to side, circumambulate deosil to south, face Altar. Take Rod and make counter-clockwise circle over dagger, saying:

By the power of Yah, the Yod of Tetragrammaton and the Wand of Will, I exorcise this dagger and free it of all contamination and negative influence. Hekas! Hekas! Este Bibeloi! Be far from here, O ye profane! I declare this dagger to be virgin.

Replace Rod. Turn to Censer, put incense into it and cense the Altar. Replace Censer, go to east, face Altar, spread hands over dagger, and say:

Yod He Vau He!
Raphael! Raphael! Raphael!
Chassan! Chassan! Chassan!

Pick up dagger, touch its point to flame of candle and say:

And thou who governest the fiery realms of Air!

Touch point of dagger to water in Cup and say:

And thou who governest the realms of fluid Air!

Touch point of dagger to rose and say:

And thou who governest the realms of pure and permeating Air!

Touch point of dagger to salt and say:

And thou who governest the denser realms of Air!

Dagger lying in both hands stretched out before you, say:

Endow this dagger with hidden forces and occult virtues so that I may be enabled with it to perform aright those magical operations for which I now dedicate it.

Hold dagger point up between upward pointing hands, breathe on it and say:

I dedicate you, Dagger, to the performance of true Magic!

Replace Dagger, circumambulate to south, face Altar, take Rod and make Circled Cross over Dagger, saying:

I charge you with energy! Be potent! Be powerful! Be sharp!

Replace Rod. Continue deosil to west, face Altar, dip fingers into water of Cup and sprinkle a few drops on Dagger, saying:

But power must be balanced by mercy. Be ye merciful!

Take Dagger and offer it by holding it high in both hands, saying:

Lord of Air! This is thy Instrument. Use it and me.

Replace Dagger. Go to seat, sit. Perform Closing Exercises of Temple Rite.

DAGGER MAGIC

The DAGGER, or the SWORD, is the third of the four instruments, tools or weapons of Magic and is associated with the Vau of Tetragammaton and the Element of Air. It represents the LIFE-FORCE of the Magician or Theurgist, his ANALYTICAL FACULTY, his REASON, his BREATH, his MIND.

Telepathy

To send a thought to another person:

Beginning in the west and holding Dagger upright in right hand, circumambulate deosil bare Altar one and a half times, stopping in the east. Place Dagger in center of Altar pointing west, spin it, saying:

(Name of Person) Dagger, Dagger, make it clear. What direction is he (she) from here?

After Dagger stops spinning, continue deosil around Altar until you come to the hilt of the Dagger. Crouch there, take hold of the hilt with right hand, call aloud the name of the person three times and repeat aloud three times the definite thought you wish that person to receive. Then visualize the Dagger flying as an arrow but with the speed of a bullet, carrying the thought and penetrating it into the mind of the person. Will it with such intensity that you almost (or do) break out into a sweat, and feel exhausted afterward. Finally, carrying Dagger, circumambulate widdershins.

Another technique of doing the same thing:

Dagger and Cup with water on Altar. Deosil circumambulation. Charge Cup with name and likeness of person you wish to receive the thought. Hold Dagger blade to lips, whispering three times the thought. Then slowly, carefully, deliberately touch point of Dagger to surface of water and insert it beyond the spot where your lips touched the blade, willing with great intensity that thought to enter that person's mind. Same sweat, same exhaustion as above. Fling the water through an open window or door into the air. Re-charge Cup with your love and cleanse Dagger by wiping it with a clean cloth. No widdershins circumambulation necessary.

Psychic Surgery

Begin this by magically removing a wart from another person. Without touching the skin, carefully make a widdershins circle about the wart with point of Dagger, saying:

Let the offering be without blemish.
Hekas! Hekas! Este Bibeloi!

24

Be far from here, O ye profane!
Begone, thou blemish, begone!

Within a week the wart will disappear. It is the acceptance by the other person that does much of the work, therefore it is important that you assume the attitude of authority, the "air" of "one who can." After you have demonstrated success with warts, experiment with freckles, "sty on the eye," fever blisters, and other minor blemishes. In psychic surgery never touch the skin.

Healing By Breath

To remove or relieve the pain of a burn:

Bend close so that your breath is upon burned area as you say:

And the Lord said unto Satan, The Lord rebuke thee, O Satan; even the Lord that hath chosen Jerusalem rebuke thee; is not this a brand plucked out of the fire! (Zechariah 3:2)

Blow gently and cooly upon the burned area. Then make gentle passes over the area with hand (touching not the skin) and shake hand as if flinging water from the fingers.

To stop the flow of blood:

Blow forcibly and hotly upon the wound, saying mentally: "And when I passed by thee and saw thee polluted in thine own blood, I said unto thee when thou wast in thy blood, Live! Yea, I said unto thee when thou wast in thy blood, Live!" (Ezekiel 16:6)

Healing by breathing upon the afflicted area of the body is a very ancient practice and experiments along this line may now be begun by the Theurgist if he is so inclined. But presume not to take the place of the Medical Doctor.

Chanting

The Neophyte should purchase a record or tape of GREGORIAN chants and play it many times. This will familiarize you of the technique and method of chanting. Intoning and chanting should be practiced. A deep resonant monotone with occasional changes of pitch or key is to be sought for, found and practiced, half singing, half speaking. Some Theurgists prefer a high-pitched, almost shrill voice, but most like to lower the pitch of their voice to a vibrant bass or alto. The tone is magically effective when it produces a vibration that can be felt in the palms of the hands or the soles of the feet.

THE DIVINE PHYSICIAN

Moon waxing is an Air Sign.

On Altar are Rod in south, Cup with water in west, Dagger in east, coin or salt in north. Censer with appurtances and material on stand in south. The incense is Galbanum or mixture of Rose Petals and Lavendar. Chair in west.

Perform Opening Exercises of Temple Rite.

After entering the Silence, stand, go deosil to south and cense Altar, return to west, sit. Read aloud:

An open gateway in the heavens with stars above and below. Beyond the gate a pleasant meadow is abloom with fragrant flowers. In the gateway a radiant Angel stands leaning on a traveler's staff. His robe shimmers in irridescence, a bright short sword and a flask of healing ointment fastened to his belt. A gentle breeze is wafted from behind him. Upon the starry threshold is his name: Raphael, "God has healed."

Become utterly still for a moment. Then, in the east, visualize a vast Angelic figure, conceived of in the traditional, conventional style, coloring that of a glorious sunrise. Adore in silence.

From behind Raphael should be felt a gentle breeze growing into a gust of wind which, permeating the entire body, blows from it every trace of impurity and heals every wound.

Stand. Raise right arm to an angle of forty-five degrees, saying:

I salute Raphael, "God has healed," Angel of Truth, Archangel of Air, Regent of the East, Instructor of Mankind, the Divine Physician.

Return arm to side. Then make a Sign of Air: Stretch both arms upwards and outwards, the elbows bent at right angles, hands bent backward, palms upwards, as if supporting a weight. Say:

Raphael! Healer of Wounds! Greater Hierophant of the Mysteries! Thanks be to thee for thy healing and thy truth.

Sit. Perform Closing Exercises of Temple Rite. If possible, have record or tape playing Wagner's "Liebestrod" or Mendelssohn's "Spring Song" or other music suggestive of Air.

This rite should be repeated (a.) whenever a physical or non-physical wound needs healing, (b.) before a major journey, and (c.) on the Feast of Raphael, October 24.

THE DISK OF EARTH

The Elemental Instrument, Tool or Weapon of Earth is the Disk, the Pentacle, the Coin, the Shield. This is a round disc of wood, metal, stone or baked clay, about four inches in diameter and from one-half inch to one inch in thickness, nicely polished, and truly circular, and of even thickness. There should be a circular white or cream colored border and a hexagram of the same color in the center of each face of the disc. The space within the border should be divided into four compartments by two diameters at right angles. These four compartments are to be colored: the upper, Citrine; right, Olive Green; left, Russet; lowest, Black. The Divine Name ADONAI HA ARETZ, the Archangelic Name AURIEL, and the symbols of Taurus, Virgo and Capricorn should be written and drawn in black round the white or cream border. The design should be the same on both sides of the disc.

If you possibly can make the whole thing yourself, by all means do so. If not, get a woodworker to turn one out on a lathe and paint it yourself.

Or if you know someone who works in ceramics, order one made to the above specifications. A disc of solid lead would be ideal, its heavy weight would be most suggestive of earth. At the least, but serviceable, a wood or metal circular box or can top will do, provided the design is painted on. Wash, rinse, dry and polish the disc before you consecrate it.

In ceremonial working the Disk should be held in the hand with the citrine uppermost unless there is a special reason for using one of the other compartments. And in this matter remember that citrine is the airy part of Earth, russet the fiery, olive the watery, black the earthy part of Earth.

Moon approaching the Full and in an Earth Sign.

On Altar are the new Disk in the center, Rod and candle in south, Cup with water in west, Dagger in east and dish of salt in the north. Censer and incense on stand in the south. The incense is Dittany of Crete. Chair in west.

Perform Opening Exercises of Temple Rite.

Stand. Say the "Holy art thou" prayer. Go to south, exorcise the Disk and cense the Altar. Continue deosil to north, face Altar, spread hands over Disk and say:

> Adonai ha Aretz!
> Auriel! Auriel! Auriel!
> Phorlakh! Phorlakh! Phorlakh!

Pick up Disk with right hand. Touch russet compartment of Disk to flame and say:

> And thou who rulest the fiery essence of Earth!

Dip third or ring finger of left hand to water in Cup and touch olive compartment of Disk, saying:

> And thou who rulest the moist and fluid essences of Earth.

Shift Disk from right to left hand. With right hand take Dagger and touch its point to the citrine portion of the Disk and say:

> And thou who rulest the airy and delicate essences of Earth!

Touch a grain or two of salt to the black portion of the Disk and say:

> And thou who rulest the dense and solid Earth!

Elevate the Disk with both hands stretched upward, saying:

> Endow this Disk with hidden forces and occult virtues so that I may be enabled with it to perform aright those magical operations for which I now dedicate it.

Place Disk on northern section of Altar, cover it with salt, press on it with both hands, saying:

> I dedicate you, Disk, to the performance of true Magic! Be solid! Be stable! Be strong!

With second finger make Circled Cross over Disk and say:

> Demeter! Gaia! Ceres! Fam'd,
> August, the source of wealth and various nam'd;
> Great nurse, all-bounteous, blessed and divine,
> Who joy'st in peach; this Disk is thine!
> Bless it and me!

Go to west, sit. Perform Closing Exercises of Temple Rite.

27

OF THE EARTH, EARTHY

The DISK or the PENTACLE is the fourth of the four instruments, tools or weapons of Magic and is associated with the final He of Tetragrammaton and the Element of Earth. It represents the MATTER of the Magician or Theurgist, his MASS, his INERTIA, his LAW, his BODY. For us in the physical body Earth is the strongest of the Elements, more enduring in its static depths than the rages of Fire or the terrors of Water, even if less dramatic than the menaces of Air. Out of the Earth our physical bodies came, to it they go back. We usually take Earth to signify our state of "stable solidity" as we have accustomed ourselves to living more on its rate of vibration than that of the other Elements. But they are just as "real" as Earth and a truly meaningful life depends upon the proportional balance of each of the four Elements in a "rounded" or "whole" individuation. There is a mistaken impression among many occult students that they should eliminate Earth in order to become truly spiritual. Let those who attempt this do so to their own peril, for by so doing they create a state of imbalance and "unbalanced force is evil, evil is unbalanced force.."

GRAVITY and MAGNETISM are the two great Earth-forces. These are necessary magically as well as materially so we must establish and maintain Earth-contacts when and while we are dealing with Inner as well as Outer-forces and energies.

AURIEL is the Archangel of Earth. He is said to be "the Lord of Awe," inspiring a sense of deepest respect for the wonders of creation, and he can put the "fear of God" into human hearts. Those who have experienced natural cataclysms and disasters such as earthquakes and avalanches well know just how terrifying Auriel can be. On the other hand Earth may be peaceful and wonderful. Most of us have lost contact with its natural power and beauty since we spend most of our time among the artifacts we have made from the Earth. The Theurgist should seek Earth contacts by frequent returns to Nature with long walks in the country, dancing barefoot on sandy beach or dewy grass, digging a garden, etc., as well as by eating organic and natural foods. There is much to learn about absorbing energies from Earth at source and Auriel has the means of teaching us.

All physical things are made from Earth of one kind or another and every Plane of Existence has its own particular sort of Earth which can be adapted in equivalent ways once we learn the secrets of handling it. This is why we must seek the acquaintance of Auriel who links our consciousness with Earth so that we may penetrate its secrets and enter its marvelous treasure-house.

LIGHT OF GOD

Waxing Moon in an Earth Sign.

On Altar are Rod in south, Cup with water in west, Dagger in east, Disk in north. Censer on stand in south. Incense is Dittany of Crete. One chair in west, one in south.

Perform Opening Exercises of Temple Rite.

Stand, go to south, cense Altar. Sit in south. Read aloud:

An open gateway in the heavens with stars above and below. Beyond the gate a high craggy mountain towers upward in dark sky where the Aurora Borealis glows in radiant light. Within the gateway a glorious Angel stands. Cradled in his left arm is the Book of the Law. From his upraised right hand fall blessings that take the form of flowers as they fall. Upon the threshold stars is writ his name: Auriel, Light of God.

Become utterly still for a moment. Then, in the north, vividly visualize a vast Angelic figure, conceived of in the conventional traditional way. The colors are citrine, russet, olive, with touches of black. The northern lights streak upward behind him. Adore in silence.

An emanation of great strength should be sensed coming from the Archangel. And the northern lights should play within, creating a curious but wonderful kind of inner illumination.

Stand. Raise right arm to an angle of forty-five degrees and say:

I salute Auriel, Light of God, Prince of Heaven, Archangel of Earth, Regent of the North, Lord of Awe, Teacher of the Law and Giver of Experience.

Return arm to side. Then make Sign of Earth: Advance the right foot, stretch out the right hand upward and forward, the left hand downward and backward, palms open. Afterwards, say:

Praise ever be to Auriel for his strength and his understanding.

Return to west, sit. Perform Closing Exercises of Temple Rite. If possible have a record or tape of Beethoven's "Ninth Symphony" playing during the rite.

This ceremony should be repeated (a.) whenever there is special need for great strength, (b.) whenever a bitter or disastrous experience needs to be spiritually comprehended, and (c.) on April 24th, the Feast of Auriel.

THE TAROT

The Tarot is a book of seventy-eight pages made in the form of a pack of seventy-eight cards. In Magic, Tarot is pronounced TAY-roh.

The Major Arcana

Twenty-two cards comprise the Major Arcana. They are called Atu, Keys, and Trumps Major. Of these, twenty-one are numbered, one is unnumbered.

Atu O. THE FOOL or Mate or The Vagabond. The Holy Innocent.

Atu I. THE MAGICIAN or The Juggler, The Magus of Power, The Juggler with the Secret of the Universe.

Atu II. THE HIGH PRIESTESS or Pope Joan, The Priestess of the Silver Star.

Atu III. THE EMPRESS. The Daughter of the Mighty Ones. The Woman Clothed with the Sun.

Atu IV. THE EMPEROR. Son of The Morning, Chief Among the Mighty.

Atu V. THE HIEROPHANT or The Pope. The Magus of the Eternal.

Atu VI. THE LOVERS or The Twins or Temptation. The Children of the Voice. The Oracle of the Mighty Gods.

Atu VII. THE CHARIOT. The Lord of the Triumph of Light. The Child of the Powers of the Waters.

Atu VIII. JUSTICE or Truth or Adjustment. The Daughter of the Lords of Truth.

Atu IX. THE HERMIT. The Prophet of the Eternal. The Magus of the Voice of Power.

Atu X. THE WHEEL OF FORTUNE. The Lord of the Forces of Life.

Atu XI. STRENGTH or Power. The Daughter of the Flaming Sword.

Atu XII. THE HANGED MAN. The Redeemer in the Waters.

Atu XIII. DEATH. The Child of the Great Transformers. Lord of the Gate of Death.

Atu XIV. TEMPERANCE or Art or Time. The Daughter of the Reconcilers. The Bringer Forth of Life.

Atu XV. THE DEVIL. The Lord of the Gates of Matter. The Child of the Forces of Time.

Atu XVI. THE TOWER or The Lightning Struck Tower. The Fortress of the Most High. The House of God. The Fire of Heaven.

Atu XVII. THE STAR or The Stars. The Daughter of the Firmament. The Dweller between the Waters.

Atu XVIII. THE MOON or The Waning Moon. The Ruler of Flux and Reflux. The Child of the Sons of the Mighty.

Atu XIX. THE SUN. The Lord of the Fire of the World.

Atu XX. JUDGMENT or The Resurrection of the Dead or The Angel or The Last Judgment. The Spirit of the Primal Fire.

Atu XXI. THE UNIVERSE or The World. The Great One of the Night of Time.

The Minor Arcana

Fifty-six cards comprise the Minor Arcana. These are formed of four series of fourteen cards each.

The four series, each of which is called a Suit, are:

THE SUIT OF WANDS, or Sceptres, or Rods, representing the Element Fire and the Yod of Tetragrammaton.

THE SUIT OF CUPS, or Goblets, or Chalices, representing the Element of Water and the first He of Tetragrammaton.

THE SUIT OF SWORDS, or Daggers, or Knives, representing the Element Air and the Vau of Tetragrammaton.

THE SUIT OF PENTACLES, or Coins, or Disks, representing the Element Earth and the final He of Tetragrammaton.

The Royalty

The four Court cards of each suit are:

THE KNIGHT, the Prince, or the Emperor. Fire. Yod.

THE QUEEN. Water. First He.

THE KING. Air. Vau.

THE PAGE, or the Princess. Earth. Final He.

Each royal personage has a title.

The Aces

The first or one card of each suit is called an Ace. The four aces represent the root-force of the four Elements:

THE ACE OF WANDS is "the Root of the Powers of Fire."

THE ACE OF CUPS is "the Root of the Powers of Water."

THE ACE OF SWORDS is "the Root of the Powers of Air."

THE ACE OF PENTACLES is "the Root of the Powers of Earth."

The Decanate Cards

The smaller cards of the four suits, thirty-six in number, answer unto the thirty-six decans of the Zodiac.

The Wands

The two card is called the Deuce. The Deuce of Wands is LORD OF DOMINION. Aries 0° to 10°.

The three card is called the Trey. The Trey of Wands is LORD OF ESTABLISHED STRENGTH, Aries 11° to 20°.

The Four of Wands is LORD OF PERFECTED WORK. Aries 21° to 30°. (We remember that the 30th degree of one Sign is 0° of the next.)

Five of Wands is LORD OF STRIFE. Leo 0° to 10°.

Six of Wands is LORD OF VICTORY. Leo 11° to 20°.

Seven of Wands is LORD OF VALOR. Leo 21° to 30°.

Eight of Wands is LORD OF SWIFTNESS. Sagittarius 0° to 10°.

Nine of Wands is LORD OF GREAT STRENGTH. Sagittarius 11° to 20°.

Ten of Wands is LORD OF OPPRESSION. Sagittarius 21° to 30°.

Cups

Deuce of Cups is the LADY OF LOVE. First Decan of Cancer.

Trey of Cups is the LADY OF ABUNDANCE. Second Decan of Cancer.

Four of Cups is the LADY OF BLENDED PLEASURE. Third Decan of Cancer.

Five of Cups is the LADY OF LOSS OF PLEASURE. First Decan of Scorpio.

Six of Cups is the LADY OF PLEASURE. Second Decan of Scorpio.

Seven of Cups is the LADY OF ILLUSIONARY SUCCESS. Third Decano of Scorpio.

Eight of Cups is the LADY OF ABANDONED SUCCESS. First Decan of Pisces.

Nine of Cups is the LADY OF MATERIAL SUCCESS and the Wish Card. Second Decan of Pisces.

Ten of Cups is the LADY OF PERFECTED SUCCESS. Third Decan of Pisces.

Swords

Deuce of Swords is MASTER OF PEACE RESTORED. First Decan of Libra.

Trey of Swords is MASTER OF SORROW. Second Decan of Libra.

Four of Swords is MASTER OF REST FROM STRIPE. Third Decan of Libra.

Five of Swords is MASTER OF DEFEAT. First Decan of Aquarius.

Six of Swords is MASTER OF EARNED SUCCESS. Second Decan of Aquarius.

Seven of Swords is MASTER OF UNSTABLE EFFORT. Third Decan of Aquarius.

Eight of Swords is MASTER OF SHORTENED FORCE. First Decan of Gemini.

Nine of Swords is MASTER OF DESPAIR AND CRUELTY. Second Decan of Gemini.

Ten of Swords is MASTER OF RUIN. Third Decan of Gemini.

Pentacles

Deuce of Pentacles is MAID OF HARMONIOUS CHANGE. First Decan of Capricorn.

Trey of Pentacles is MAID OF MATERIAL WORKS. Second Decan of Capricorn.

Four of Pentacles is MAID OF EARTHLY POWER. Third Decan of Capricorn.

Five of Pentacles is MAID OF MATERIAL TROUBLE. First Decan of Taurus.

Six of Pentacles is MAID OF MATERIAL SUCCESS. Second Decan of Taurus.

Seven of Pentacles is MAID OF SUCCESS UNFULFILLED. Third Decan of Taurus.

Eight of Pentacles is MAID OF PRUDENCE. First Decan of Virgo.

Nine of Pentacles is MAID OF MATERIAL GAIN. Second Decan of Virgo.

Ten of Pentacles is MAID OF WEALTH. Third Decan of Virgo.

CONSECRATION OF THE WHEEL OF THE TAROT

When the Moon is waxing, consecrate your Pack of Tarot Cards, having previously wiped every one of them, front and back, with a clean cloth. Take the Major Arcana with the Fool on top and the others in consecutive order underneath and holding them tightly in both hands twist to move slightly clockwise the cards so as to make a "rose" of them, every card being partially exposed. Put this "rose" on the center of the Altar. In the south, arrange the Court cards of the Wand suit, right to left, Knight, Queen. King, Page. Below the Page, place the Ace of Wands. Below the Ace and along the edge of the Altar, right to left, place the decanate cards of the Wand suit, Two to Ten. In the space in line with the Ace and between the Court cards and the decanate cards, place the Rod with male, end resting on the Ace.

Arrange the cards of the other suits similarly, Cups in the west with Cup containing water, Pentacles in the north with Disk, and Swords in the east with Dagger. The cards may be arranged in arcs so as to give to the whole arrangement the appearance of a large wheel covering the top of the Altar with the cluster of the Major Arcana in the center. Incense is a mixture of equal parts of Frankincense, Myrrh, Galbanum (or Rose Petals and Lavender) and Dittany of Crete. Chair in west.

Perform Opening Exercises of Temple Rite.

Stand, go to south, face Altar. Without touching them, make sweeping gestures over cards from center outward with both hands, as if sweeping them clean of all impurities, saying:

> By the Holy Tetragrammaton, Yod, He, Vau, He; I exorcise all influences of evil and error that they may be banished and driven forth from these Tarot cards. Hekas! Hekas! Este Bibeloi! Be far from here, O ye profane, for a sacred rite of Magic is about to take place.

Cense Altar. Then circumambulate deosil three complete circuits of the Altar. Returned to the south, face Altar, take Rod and make Circled Cross over cluster of Major Arcana and say:

> Yod! Fire! Khabs Am Pekht! Konx Om Pax! Light in Extension. May the LIGHT of the Mysteries be contained herein.

(Note: "Khabs Am Pekht" is ancient Egyptian and the original of the Greek "Konx Om Pax" which was uttered at the Eleusinian Mysteries. Both sentences mean "Light in extension" or "Light rushing out in one ray," signifying the light of the truth of man's own divinity illuminating his consciousness.)

Beginning at the right, touch with Rod each of the Wand Court cards and say:

> Sir Knight, I invest you Lord of the Flame and the Lightning.

> Gracious Lady of the Rainbow, I invest you Queen of the Thrones of Flames.

Lion-hearted King, I invest you Prince of the Chariots of Fire.
Fiery Page, I invest you Princess of the Shining Flame.

Touch Rod to Ace and say:

Ace of Wands, you are the Root of the Powers of Fire. Assign your Lords their appointed tasks.

Replace Rod. Take the Ace of Wands and touch it face to face to each Wand decanate card from the Deuce to the Ten. If you can, name each card by its proper title, as Lord of Dominion, Lord of Established Strength, etc. Otherwise, do it silently. Replace Ace.

Go to west. With Cup make Circled Cross over Major Arcana, saying:

He! Water! Khabs Am Pekht! Konx Om Pax! Light in Extension. May the LOVE of the Mysteries be contained herein.

Beginning at the right, hold Cup over each of the Cup Court cards and say:

Sir Knight, I invest you Lord of the Waves and the Waters.
Gracious Lady of the Lake, I invest you Queen of the Thrones of the Waters.
Noble King of the Rivers, I invest you Prince of the Chariots of Water.
Sweet Lady of the Mist, I invest you Princess of the Waters.

Hold Cup over Ace and say:

Ace of Cups, you are the Root of the Powers of Water. Assign your Ladies their appointed tasks.

Replace Cup. Take Ace of Cups and touch it face to face to each Cup decanate card from the Deuce to the Ten. Name each card as it is touched or do it silently. Replace Ace.

Circumambulate to east. Take Dagger and make Circled Cross over Major Arcana, saying:

Vau! Air! Khabs Am Pekht! Konx Om Pax! Light in Extension. May the LIFE of the Mysteries be contained herein.

Touch point of Dagger to the Sword Court cards and say:

Sir Knight, I invest you Lord of the Winds and Breezes.

Gracious Lady of the Breeze, I invest you Queen of the Thrones of Air.

Royal Giver of Life and Death, I invest you Prince of the Chariots of the Winds.

Airy Page of Swords, I invest you Princess of the Rushing Winds.

Touch point of Dagger to Ace and say:

Ace of Swords, you are the Root of the Powers of Air. Assign your Masters their appointed tasks,

Replace Dagger. Take Ace of Swords and touch it face to face to each Sword decanate card from the Deuce to the Ten. Name each card as it is touched, or do it silently. Replace Ace.

Circumambulate deosil to north. Take Disk and make Circled Cross over the Major Arcana, saying:

He! Earth! Khabs Am Pekht! Konx Om Pax! Light in extension.

May the LAW of the Mysteries be contained herein.

Hold Disk over each Pentacle Court card and say:

Sir Knight, I invest you Lord of the Wide and Fertile Land.

Gracious Lady of the Mountain, I invest you Queen of the Thrones of Earth.

Royal Curator of the Earth's Treasures, I invest you Prince of the Chariots of Earth.

Stable Page of Pentacles, I invest you Princess of the Echoing Hills.

Hold Disk over Ace and say:

Ace of Pentacles, you are the Root of the Powers of Earth. Assign your Maidens to their appointed tasks.

Replace Disk. Take Ace of Pentacles and touch it face to face to each Pentacle decanate card from the Deuce to the Ten. Name each card as it is touched or do it silently. Replace Ace.

Go deosil to west. Lift both hands to shoulder height and say:

In the Divine Name IAO, I invoke thee thou great angel HRU (huh-ROO) who art set over the operations of this Secret Wisdom.

Sit. Gather up the cards, all in one pile, put both hands on them and say:

Lay thy hands invisibly upon these cards of the Tarot that thereby I may obtain true knowledge of hidden things. Khabs Am Pekht! Knox Om Pax! Light in Extension. I dedicate you, Tarot, to the performance of true Magic. Reveal! Instruct! Prophesy!

Sit back, relax. Enter the Silence.

Perform Closing Exercises of Temple Rite.

THE PATH OF THE SERPENT

Place Tarot Atu II, the High Priestess, upright, before you.

Close your eyes and enter the Silence.

Open your eyes and gaze at the Atu before you for five minutes.

Perform this meditation three days in succession. Do it three times, but only three times, before proceeding further. And spend only five minutes each time in quiet and attentive gazing at the Atu. Some remarkable subjective phenomena are apt to occur. After each period, perform Closing Exercises of Temple Rite.

Proceed by repeating the meditation with each of the Tarot Atu. Spend just three days on each Atu.

After the High Priestess, the Atu are to be considered in this order:

Atu XVII, the Star; Atu XVIII, the Waning Moon; Atu XV, the Devil; Atu IV, the Emperor; Atu XIX, the Sun; Atu XIV, Temperance; Atu I, the Magician; Atu XVI, the Tower; Atu III, the Empress; Atu IX, the Hermit; Atu X, the Wheel of Fortune; Atu XI, Strength; Atu VI, the Lovers; Atu VII, the Chariot; Atu V, the Hierophant; Atu VIII, Justice; Atu XXI, the Universe; Atu XX, the Judgment; Atu XII, the Hanged Man; Atu 0, the Fool.

ROSH CHODESH

Rite of the New Moon

In center of Altar is a Holy Bible with a white rose or other pale flower marking the place of Psalm 104, or such flowers may be in a vase beside the open Bible. Rod and candle in the south. In west is Cup with a pale or white wine such as sherry, chablis or sauterne. In north are Disk and a small plate or saucer with small piece of a doughnut or a cookie whose ingredients include flour and oil. In east are Dagger, a small brass or copper bowl, and a small sheet of white paper on which previously has been copied in red Numbers 28:11 to 14 and the Magical Intention (what is planned or hoped to be accomplished magically) for the coming month. Censer on side table in the south with charcoal, container of Dittany of Crete incense, lighter or matches and ashtray. Ritual Book on stand by chair in the west.

Opening Exercises of Temple Rite, igniting the charcoal when lighting the candle and censing the Altar after the Sign of the Enterer.

Seated in the west, facing east, read aloud:

> The Moon is new, pale crescent in the sky. Fair is she, the many-named virgin. But the name with her number is Levannah. Her lord the Sun kisses her in conjunction. The bridegroom knows his bride. Fertile is she, fruitful will she be. Now her light will increase, growing brighter night by night. What is begun when the Moon is new is fructified and given increase. My Magical Intention for this month is . . . (here name those projects and plans you have in mind for the month at hand) . . . I seek a blessing on this.

Stand and say:

> Shaddai El Chai (shod-DOY el hoy) Almighty Living God! Happy are they that dwell in thy house; they will be ever praising thee. Happy is the people that is thus favored, happy is the people whose God is the Lord. O Lord, open thou my lips and my mouth shall declare thy praise. (Repeat Psalm Twenty-three while circumambulating deosil, returning to west to say:) Blessed art thou, O Lord our God, who bestowest loving kindness and art master of all things. Thou art holy and thy name is holy, and holy beings praise thee daily. Blessed art thou, O Lord, Shaddai El Chai, Almighty Living God!

Go to Altar, take the Bible and read aloud Psalm 104. Close and kiss the Bible and return it to its place, saying:

> I rejoice in the service of the sanctuary and in the songs of David.

Go from west to north to east. Take Dagger, breathe on it, and with its point touch the small piece of white paper, then replace Dagger. Now take the paper and set fire to it from the burning candle, holding it for a moment while burning, then dropping it into the copper or brass bowl, saying:

> Upon Beth-El, the Altar of Zion, I present the burnt offering of the New Moon. I do this in commemoration of ancient practice. And believing in the essential goodness of the Great Ones behind our being, I present my Magical Intention through the portals of fire and air. With faith, in confidence, I ask their aid in this.

Go to the south, take up Rod, point its male end upward with upstretched arm and say:

O thou single Source of Light and Life whose scattered seeds we are on earth, renew this month unto us for good and for blessing, for joy and gladness, for salvation and consolation, for support and sustenance, for life and peace, for guidance and progression on the Path of Light that leads to at-one-ment with thee!

Replace Rod. Go to west, take up Cup and say:

The pale wine of the New Moon. Clean it is, dry and virginal, refreshing and provocative.

Take Cup of wine to north, set it beside the plate with doughnut or cookie. Take Disk and with it touch the cake, saying:

The sacrifical flour and oil are properly balanced in the Cake of Light. The Holy Guardian Angel is attained by self-sacrifice and discipline.

Replace Disk. With right forefinger make Circled Cross over cake and wine, saying:

May the Mighty Ones bless this food and drink to my service and me to theirs. My Magical Intention for this month is . . . May this oblation fortify me to accomplish this purpose.

Eat the cake. Drink the wine. Pause in contemplation. Then return deosil to seat in west.

Perform Closing Exercises of Temple Rite.

Lunar Cakes of Light

Mix 1 tablespoon honey, 1/3 cup vegetable oil, 1/2 cup brown sugar, 1 tablespoon white wine. Add 1 1/2 cups flour, 1/4 teaspoon baking soda, 1/2 teaspoon salt, 1/2 teaspoon cinnamon, 1/2 teaspoon allspice, 1/2 teaspoon ground cardamon, 1 drop blood, 1 1/4 cups oatmeal. Combine well, adding water if necessary to make into rollable dough. Roll thin on floured board, cut into small crescent-shaped cakes and bake in preheated oven at 350 degrees about 15 minutes until light brown.

THE ESBAT

Full Moon Ceremony

On Altar is Cup with white wine. A bell whose tone is soft and silvery is on side table by chair in west or may be carried by an acolyte. A bouquet of white or pale (pastel) flowers in a low vase may also be on Altar. If others are to be present, their chairs are behind or on either side of that of the Theurgist in the west. When and if possible the Full Moon Ceremony should be performed outdoors on the shore of a body of water, using a boulder or stone as the Altar.

If possible, enter from north or west. Salute Altar as in Temple Rite, take three steps foward, stop, bow low from waist, straighten, go to west, sit. (Others will follow with same procedure.)

The bell is rung once. Read aloud:

The time of the Full Moon draws near. The Moon is full! Full Moon is here! Priest and Priestess, Seeress and Seer—Pray to the Lady, for she will hear!

Pray to the Moon when she is round;
Luck with you shall then abound—
What you seek for shall be found
In sea or sky or solid ground.

The bell is rung three times. Stand and intone:

Hear, Goddess queen, diffusing silver light,
Bull-horn'd and wand'ring thro' gloom of night.

With stars surrounded, and with circuit wide
Night's torch extending, through the heav'ns you ride;
Female and male, with silv'ry rays you shine,
And now full-orbed, now tending to decline.
Mother of ages, fruit-producing Moon,
Whose amber orb makes Night's reflected noon;
Lover of horses, splendid queen of night,
All-seeing pow'r, bedecked with starry light,
Lover of vigilance, the foe of strife,
In peace rejoicing, and a prudent life;
Fair lamp of night, its ornament and friend,
Who giv'st to Nature's works their destined end.
Queen of the stars, all-wise Diana, hail!
Deck'd with a graceful robe and ample veil.
Come, blessed Goddess, prudent, starry, bright,
Come, moony-lamp, with chaste and splendid light.
Shine on these sacred rites with prosp'rous rays,
And pleas'd, accept thy suppliant's mystic praise.

Sit. Pause. The bell is rung five times. Then read aloud:

The Temple of Isis is built of black marble and hung with silver, and she herself sitteth veiled in the innermost. She is all goddesses that men's hearts have worshipped, for they are not many things, but one thing under many forms. She is the Anima Mundi, the Soul of the World and Source of Sleep. She is the lady of ten-thousand appellations, the many-named Maiden and Matron. Men have worshipped her as Artemis, Diana, Luna, Aradia, Habondia, Binah, Ge. Those who adore the Isis of Nature adore her as Hathor with the horns upon her brow; but those who adore the celestial Isis know her as Levannah, the Moon. She is all ancient and forgotten things wherein our roots are cast. Upon earth she is ever-fecund; in heaven she is ever-virgin. She is also the Great Deep whence life arose. She is mistress of the tides that flow and ebb and flow and never cease. In these things are the keys to her mystery.

Pause. Silently and wordlessly contemplate what has been read. The bell is sounded seven times. Slowly stand, raise both arms outward, slightly above level of shoulders, elbows bent, forearms straight up, hands bent backward, palms up, head thrown back. Then say:

O thou most holy and adorable Isis, who in the heavens art the Supernal Mother, and upon earth Our Lady of Nature, and in the airy kingdoms between heaven and earth the everchanging Moon, ruling the tides of flux and reflux upon the earth and in the hearts of men: Thee, I (we) adore in the symbol of the Moon in her splendor, ever-changing; And in the symbol of the opening of the gates of life. We see thee crowned in silver in the heavens and clad in green upon the earth, and in thy robe of many colors at the gates. O heavenly silver that answereth to the celestial gold! O green that riseth from the grey! O rainbow glory of living!

The bell is rung nine times. Begin deosil circumambulation dance while singing, chanting or saying:

Dance down the Moon, dance the Moon down,
Turning and twisting, stamping the ground.

Lovely Lady, Lovely Lady, Lovely Lady of Light!
I (we) love thee, I (we) adore thee, I (we) bless thee this night!

Charge me (us) with power, thy power so great
It livens me (us), enlightens me (us), tells me (us) my (our) fate.

Great Mother, Great Mother, Great Mother of all:
Give heed, dear Mother, give heed as I (we) call.

Bless me (us), protect me (us), lend me (us) thine aid—
Fruitful yet virgin, thou Mother, thou Maid!

Lovely Lady, Lovely Lady, Lovely Lady of Light!
I (we) love thee, I (we) adore thee, I (we) bless thee this night!

Finish dance in the west. Take Cup and lift it high with both hands, then drink. If others are present, they partake also, the Cup being passed deosil. If there is need of group action or discussion, it takes place here. Finally say:

In joy we came together. In peace let us depart,
Blessed be! (Response: Blessed be!)

If alone, conclude with Closing Exercises of Temple Rite.

FESTIVAL OF THE SPRING EQUINOX

Temple Rite of Spring

Just before dawn on the day the Sun enters Aries.

An Easter Lily or a potted spring blossoming plant is in center of Altar. At the four corners are tall white candles in candlesticks. Tarot Emperor and Ace of Wands with Rod in south. Tarot Empress, Ace of Cups, and a small brass or copper bowl are in west with Cup which contains water. Ace of Pentacles and container of salt and Disk in north. Ace of Swords and Dagger in east. On side tables are: cigarette lighter or matches with ashtray, Dittany of Crete incense (a poor but acceptable substitute is dried grass) and a Censer containing charcoal in the south; slips of paper and red pen or pencil in the west; a flower-pot containing earth, a small trowel or table knife and seeds of a spring blooming annual flower in the north; a basket or bowl of brightly colored hard-boiled eggs (a typical "Easter basket") in the east. Ritual Book on side table by chair in west. If others are to be present their chairs are on either side of that of the Theurgist in the west.

Sky-clad or robed, girded and sandled, enter Temple and salute Altar as in Opening Exercises of Temple Rite, saying:

I was glad when they said unto me,
let us go unto Beth-El.

(Others follow the Theurgist in, salute the Altar, say the opening sentence, and seat themselves in the west.)

Go deosil to south. Take lighter or matches and light the four Altar candles, southeast, southwest, northwest, northeast, saying:

Out of winter comes spring. Out of darkness comes light. Out of death comes life. Such is the law, and so mote it be!
(Response: So mote it be!)

Ignite the charcoal in the Censer, saying:

Cold has been the winter. Dormant has been the life. The banked fires of Malkuth smoulder in anticipation of the coming of her Lord the Sun.

Pause until the charcoal begins to glow. Take incense and offer it by holding it high in both hands, saying:

May the fragrance of Virgin Earth attract her Lord the Sun for she is hungry and ready for love.

Cast the incense upon the glowing charcoal, put on cover, take Censer by chains and cense the Altar with three swings left, three swings right, three swings forward, while saying:

And may my (our) thoughts, my (our) words, my (our) actions and my (our) deeds rise as fragrance to the nostrils of mine own (our) Holy Guardian Angel for I (we) too am (are) hungry and ready for love.

Replace Censer. Go to west, face Altar, raise both arms in adoration (others stand) and say:

Holy art Thou, Lord of the Universe!
Holy art Thou, whom nature hath not formed.
Holy art Thou, the vast and the mighty One,
Lord of the light and of the darkness!
IAO! IAO! IAO! (Others repeat.)

Perform the Quabalistic Cross and the Sign of the Enterer. Sit. Enter the Silence. (Others do the same.) After a while, take Ritual Book and read aloud:

Out of death comes life. Out of darkness comes light. Out of winter comes spring. Today the Sun crosses the Celestial Equator and re-enters the Northern Hemisphere as the virile young male hungry and ready for love. The Prince seeks his bride. Today the Sun enters Aries. This is the Spring Equinox, the first day of spring. Spring! A trickle of water along the edge of a ragged snow bank in the warming sunshine of March. There is promise in that gentle sound, it is the music of fields and streams. The waxen buds of the elms and the wooly fingers of the willows have a fragrance all their own. The smell of freshly turned earth, of rain drops and of grass, is in the air. Tiny pale green fires of baby vegetation gleam along the slopes. Here is Springtime and the spirit of eternal youth unquenchably aflame for living and adventure! I (we) accept it and rejoice! Time has turned full circle, bringing me (us) to youth again. I am (we are) young and fresh once more, with every opportunity of life before me (us). I arise (let us rise up) and claim my (our) birth right.

Stand. Say:

O Light Divine! Be thou my (our) life that I (we) may learn thy law of perfect love— DO WHAT THOU WILT!

(Response: In perfect love—DO WHAT THOU WILT!)

For Love is the Law, Love under Will.

(Response: Love is the Law, Love under Will.)

Go to Altar. Take Tarot Emperor and Empress and put them face together among the foliage of the potted plant and say:

The Son of the Morning and Chief Among the Mighty knows his bride and rejoices! The virgin Daughter of the Mighty Ones, Kallah the Bride, receives her lover and, becoming Malkah the Queen, rejoices! Their union is glorious! All life rejoices!

EVOHE! EVOHE! EVOHE! Ye Great Ones beyond and behind my (our) being! Ye old Ones out of the Night of Time! Spring is here! Come, rejoice with me (us), join me (us) in dancing the circle round!

Greetings to my (our) loved ones and friends in other dimensions! Spring is here! Come, rejoice with me (us), join me (us) in dancing the circle round!

Ho! Little brothers and sisters of Fire, Water, Air, Earth! Spring is here, as ye know well! Come, rejoice with me (us), join me (us) in dancing the circle round!

(Blessings, dear friends and fellow-Theurgists! Spring is here! Let us rejoice in dancing the circle round!)

Music appropriate to the season, such as Mendelssohn's "Spring Song," is played. Or a song of rejoicing, traditional or especially composed for the occasion, may be played and/or sung. Or snatches of melodies may be sung "la, la, la," or hummed. Or a poem may be said in a sing-song manner. The important thing is, dance deosil around the Altar at least three times, perhaps many times if the mood or the spirit of the occasion calls for it.

After the dance (and the others are seated) return to west. Take a slip of paper and write thereon in red the magical intention or petition for the year at hand. (Others do the same.) Say:

The Bridegroom knows his Bride! Their union is fruitful! The seed that is sown now will germinate and grow, will leaf and blossom, will bear fruit and seed of its own.

(Petitions are collected deosil and placed upon the Altar.) With petition in hand, turn to Altar and say:

O Thou Source of Light and Life whose scattered seeds we are on earth, bless thou this (these) my (our) magical intention(s) and petition(s) that it (they) may germinate, grow and prosper. TETRA-GRAMMATON ALOAH VA DAATH! (ah-LOW-ah vah dah-AHTH)

Ignite petition(s) from candle in southeast corner of Altar, allow it (them) to blaze, then drop it (them) into the brass or copper bowl, saying:

41

Believing in the essential goodness and benevolence of the Great Eternal Ones behind my (our) being, I present this (these) petition(s) to them through the portals of fire and air, with faith and in confidence.

(Response: With faith, in confidence.)

Go to north. Take pot of earth, place it on Altar, saying:

Blessed be the earth that supports our living!

Take seed and hold it high, saying:

The emblem of a seed
Shows life divine indeed.

Take trowel or knife and say:

Blessed be the tools with which we till our mother earth!

Take the bowl of ashes and say:

Blessed be the matter with which we fertilize our mother earth!
With trowel or knife mix the ashes and earth in the pot and plant the

seed while saying:

Blessed be the seed implanted in a fertile field for it will grow toward the light in strength and in beauty.

Go by east and south to west. Take up Cup and say:

Life must come through love alone.
Blessed be Water, the Element of Love!

Pour some of the water into the pot, saying:

As water was our one-time womb, and moisture is our mother-milk on earth, so may these germs implanted be bathed and nourished.

Go by north to east. Take basket or bowl of eggs and say:

Life imprisoned grows interiorly to become life free. The rainbow colors of promise invite life to come forth to its fulfillment.

Put basket of eggs on Altar, saying:

An affirmation of life. Life breaks all bounds to affirm and fulfill itself.

Crack, peel and eat an egg. Drink the water in the Cup. (Others partake deosil.)

May what I (we) have partaken sustain me (us) in my (our) affirmation of fuller life.

Go to south. Take Rod and make Circled Cross over pot, saying:

And may what I (we) have intended, petitioned and planted this sacred day germinate, grow and prosper. In the name of the wisdom, the joy, the justice and the infinite mercy of the One Eternal Spirit. Amen.

(Response: Amen.)

Hold high the Rod with male end pointing upward and say:

By the power of Yah, the Yod of Tetragrammaton and the Wand of Will, abrogated is the Password used during the Descending Signs. The Password for the next six months shall be . . . . .

With male tip of Rod touch the Ace of Wands, whispering:

Root of the Powers of Fire! The new Password is . . . . . So inform the Lords.

Go to west. With female end of Rod touch the Ace of Cups and whisper:

Root of the Powers of Water! The new Password is . . . . . So inform the Ladies.

Circumambulate to east. With male end of Rod touch the Ace of Swords. Whisper:

Root of the Powers of Air! The new Password is . . . . . So inform the Masters.

Go deosil to north. With female end of Rod touch the Ace of Pentacles and whisper:

Root of the Powers of Earth! The new password is . . . . . So inform the Maidens.

Go by east to south. Replace the Rod. Continue to the west. Face Altar and say:

The winter of rest is over. Spring is at hand and summer is ahead —a time of sowing, of tilling, of work. Whatever comes to me (us) of any lasting value must be well and truly earned by mine (our) own efforts. In order to achieve I (we) must work. So here and now let willing hands be dedicated. (Spit on right hand.) Blessed be the hand put forth with might. (Spit on left hand.) Blessed be the hand put forth with meaning. (Rub hands together vigorously.) Blessed be what I (we) must do with might and meaning that my (our) hands may hold the harvest of my (our) highest hopes.

Take three steps backward, bow from waist, turn to chair, sit. Enter the Silence. Perform Quabalistic Cross. Say HUA! while rising to feet, at the same time pushing hands upward over head then outward and downward as a diver coming up out of water. Give the Sign of Silence and salute the Altar. (Others do the same.) Put things in order, get dressed, and

Have a hearty breakfast. Blessed be!

Note: Of course, if you like, raw, uncooked, fresh fertile eggs may be used; in which case the tip of the egg is broken with the Dagger and the egg is sucked.

FESTIVAL OF THE SUMMER SOLSTICE
Midsummer Night

Whereas the word midsummer really means the middle of summer, the terms Midsummer Eve, Midsummer Night and Midsummer Day occultly refer to the evening and night before and the day of the **first** day of summer when the Sun enters the Zodiacal Sign of Cancer. These times are also called

St. John's Eve, St. John's Night and St. John's Day. In the calendar, St. John's Day is June 23. But on the evening or the night **before** the Sun locally enters Cancer, a bonfire is to be made outdoors on the highest elevation available for such.

On arriving at the scene, stand in the spot selected for the bonfire and say:

> In the name of the wisdom, the joy, the justice and the infinite mercy of the One Eternal Spirit. Amen.

As the wood is being gathered and arranged, sing or say:

> Gather I (we) the wood for burning
> At the time of season's turning.
> Happy is the time of year,
> Happy all who gather here
> To wish to all a summer bright
> Beginning here this very night.

When igniting, whisper or say:

> From fire above to fire below,
> From fire within to fire without,
> May Michael's spear from there to here
> Make the magic fire appear.
> Above, below, within, without—
> Appear, fire appear!

Lay, sit or stand back and contemplate the fire for awhile. Then, standing in the south, say:

> May the Midsummer Fire attract the Holy Ones. Evohe! Evohe! Evohe! Ye Mighty Ones and Sons of the Mighty! We herald the coming of summer! Come and dance the circle round!

> May the Midsummer Fire attract the Elder Brothers of Mankind. Hail, ye Masters and Adepts! We herald the coming of summer! Come and dance the circle round!

> May the Midsummer Fire attract my (our) friends and loved ones who have gone into Higher Dimension. Greetings (here name those of your departed friends and loved ones you wish to invite). We herald the coming of summer! Come and dance the circle round!

> May the Midsummer Fire attract the Spirits of the Elements. Ho, little brothers and sisters of Fire, Water, Air, Earth! We herald the coming of summer! Come and dance the circle round!

> May the Midsummer Fire attract men and women, boys and girls, beasts and birds, reptiles and insects, fish and plants, all forms of life everywhere in all dimensions. Hail brothers! Hail sisters! We herald the coming of summer! Come and dance the circle round!

Pause. If needed, put more wood upon the fire. Then say:

> Ye are welcome, all who gather here! Let us together adore the Lord of the Universe.
> Holy art thou, Lord of the Universe!
> Holy art thou, whom nature hath not formed.
> Holy art thou, the vast and the might One.
> Lord of the light and of the darkness!

Perform the Quabalistic Cross. Give the Sign of the Enterer. Then dance in a large circle deosil around fire while singing or chanting or saying:

May Ain Soph Aur, the Radiant Light,
Hey derry derry down, Hey derry down,
Be blessed indeed on this blessed night.
Hey derry down, derry down.

May Kether the Crown thrice blessed' be,
Hey derry derry down, Hey derry down,
By yours and you, by mine and me.
Hey derry down, derry down.

May Father and Son, eternal male,
Hey derry derry down, Hey derry down,
Of Chokmah the potent, never fail!
Hey derry down, derry down.

Great Mother, Great Mother, Great Mother dear
Hey derry derry down, Hey derry down,
Bless thy children gathered here.
Hey derry down, derry down.

May the Three in One, the One in Three,
Hey derry derry down, Hey derry down,
Forever and ever blessed' be!
Hey derry down, derry down.

Sol, Great Sun, O chief of all,
Hey derry derry down, Hey derry down,
The Sign of Cancer awaits your call!
Hey derry down, derry down.

O Crab of Cancer, watery sign,
Hey derry derry down, Hey derry down,
Welcome the coming of One so fine!
Hey derry down, derry down.

Silvery Moon, so shiny, so bright,
Hey derry derry down, Hey derry down,
Bless all who dance the dance tonight!
Hey derry down, derry down.

The fire does burn, the fire does shine,
Hey derry derry down, Hey derry down,
For you and yours, for me and mine!
Hey derry down, derry down.

May each of us become this night,
Hey derry derry down, Hey derry down,
A burning and a shining light!
Hey derry down, derry down.

Life rejoices each summer to fill,
Hey derry derry down, Hey derry down,
Grass in the meadow, trees on the hill.
Hey derry down, derry down.

Glorious Summer so shining and bright,
Hey derry derry down, Hey derry down,
You're welcome, you're welcome, you're welcome tonight!
Hey derry down, derry down.

After the dance, have a picnic, make love, sing, tell stories, play music. Then, sinking into silence, watch the fire die out. Finally, after a deep sigh of contentment, say:

> In joy we came together. In peace let us now depart, each to his own abode. Happy Summer, beloved companions, Happy Summer!

Be sure the fire is completely extinguished, stamping widdershins the embers into the ground while saying:

> Thank you, brother fire. Depart ye also in peace. Fire to heaven, ashes to earth. And so mote it be. Amen.

Temple Rite of the Summer Solstice

At or near noon on the day the Sun enters Cancer.

Altar furnishings are a yellow-flowered potted plant in center; roses or other flowers of the season in vases at the four corners; between the potted plant and the vases are four tall yellow candles in candlesticks; in south are Rod and a cigarette lighter (or matches and ashtray may be on a side table); in west are Cup with water and a stein or glass of ale or dark beer; in north are Disk and a small plate with piece of pumpernickel or rye bread; in east are Dagger and a small vial or flagon of floral perfume or eau-de-cologne. Ritual Book on side table by chair in west.

Sky-clad or robed, girded and sandaled, enter Temple and salute Altar as in Opening Exercises of Temple Rite. Go deosil to south. Take lighter or matches and light the four Altar candles, southeast, southwest, northwest, northeast. Go to west, face Altar, raise both arms in adoration and say:

> Holy art Thou, Lord of the Universe!
> Holy art Thou, whom nature hath not formed.
> Holy art Thou, the vast and the mighty One.
> Lord of the light and of the darkness!
>
> IAO! IAO! IAO!

Perform the Quabalistic Cross and the Sign of the Enterer. Sit. Take Ritual Book and read:

> This is the day the Sun enters Cancer, bringing us summer. Summer! The plum thickets, the lush grass of the meadow, the white of rolling clouds, the rioting roses, and the bird calls at dawning. They have form, color, odor and sound. The blessings of sun, clouds, rain, air, and the rich, warm brown earth. How good to dwell among these pleasant things! To be a brother to the wind and a sister to the moonlight. And over it all, and part of it, and part of me, the beautiful silence of the earth!

Enter the Silence. After a while, rise and go deosil to south of Altar. Take up Rod, point its male end upward with upstretched right arm and say:

> O Thou Single Source of Light and Life whose scattered seeds we are on earth, thanks be that I have grown and flourished in thy garden. Prosper thou, I pray, whatever further efforts I must make in thy divine direction.

Lower arm to be straight in front at shoulder height, holding Rod with male tip pointing up, and say:

How goes it with the fires of summer? The blessed heat of the Sun coaxes the life within to expansion and growth, to flowering and fruitage. And may it be so with . . . . . (here name special projects, plans and people) . . . . . and with me. (Only in rare and unusual circumstances and remembering well the Law of Karma, with Rod's male tip pointing downward, it may be added:) But heat can sear and heat can burn, heat can consume, even destroy. May it be so with . . . . . (here name those projects and plans—never people— which to you are especially inimical to general or particular welfare).

Replace Rod. Go to west, take Cup and lift it to chin le/el, saying:

Blessed be Water, the Element of Love.

Hold high the Cup and say:

Great Mother! Great Mother! Great Mother of all! Give heed, dear Mother, give heed as I call!

Replace Cup on Altar and say:

How goes it with the rains of summer? The clouds drop down refreshment from the heavens to hold, sustain and nourish life. May it be so with . . . . . and with me. (As per with fire above, it may be added:) But moisture can be withheld to life-withering dryness or fall in destructive torrents. May it be so with . . . . .

Circumambulate deosil to east. Take Dagger, point upward, and say:

The way is straight, the path is long,
While flesh is weak, but spirit strong,
We need to BE, and KNOW.
Who enters life is past recall,
For none may rise save we that fall,
ABOVE is reached BELOW.

Replace Dagger. Scatter flower petals while saying:

How blow the winds of summer? They blow our blossoms into full flowering. Air is breath and breath is life. To the outer air can carry melodious sound and fragrant odor. To the inner air can carry divine inspiration. May it be so with . . . . . and with me. (As per with fire above, taking Dagger and holding it point downward, it may be added:) But winds can howl in hurricane and tornado, carrying destruction and sudden death. May it be so with . . . . . (Replace Dagger.)

Circumambulate deosil to the north. Take up Disk and say:

Adonai ha Aretz, Lord of Earth! Blessed are the signs of summer all around us. 'Tis the time of the work of cultivation. Share with me thy wisdom, strength and patience.

Warming the Disk at a candle flame, say:

How goes it with the Earth in summer? Warm is the earth. Smiling is Mother Nature. The earth forces stabilize, make concrete in the outer, give substance to thought, and bequeath constancy and endurance. May it be so with . . . . . and with me. (As per with fire above, it may be added:) But earth can tremble and earth can quake with avalanche of destruction in its wake. May it be so with . . . . .

Replace Disk. Go to east. Take up and open vial of perfume. Say:

Fragrant are the flowers of summer. A flower gives out its perfume to the atmosphere of all the world and yet retains its own perfection for itself. So does the goodness of the Great Ones come to all of us without diminishing the single source of its supply. As our animals communicate by means of scent, and flowers by fragrance, so has the human soul an odor of its own, pervading worlds most proper to itself. Therefore I must learn to live so that I may make a pleasant perfume for the Inner Ones as I approach them. To this end I anoint myself in honor of the Blessed Ones whose company I seek this season and for evermore.

Anoint yourself while saying:

May light and beauty be upon me in the name of the wisdom (forehead), the joy (chin), the justice (right cheek), and the infinite mercy (left cheek) of the One Eternal Spirit (encircle face). Amen (under nose).

Stopper and replace vial. Go by south to west. Take ale or beer and say:

In olden times our ancestors used ale (beer) to celebrate this season since it seemed to them the blood of that beneficience which brought them barley bread.

Take the container with ale to the north, set it by the plate of bread. Touch the bread and say:

The good dark bread symbolizes the richness of the earth from which comes all our material supply.

With forefinger make Circled Cross over bread and ale, saying:

May the Mighty Ones bless this food and drink to my service and me to theirs.

Eat the bread. Drink the ale. Pause in contemplation. Then return deosil to seat in west.

Perform Closing Exercises of Temple Rite.

FESTIVAL OF THE AUTUMNAL EQUINOX

Temple Rite of the Autumnal Equinox

Near sunset on the day the Sun enters Libra.

Altar furnishings are a cornucopia or basket of fall foliage, flowers and fruit including ears of corn or a sheaf of wheat, tall orange candles set in small pumpkins or gourds at the four corners, Ace of Wands and Rod in south, Ace of Cups and Cup with cider in west, Ace of Pentacles and Disk in north and Ace of Swords and Dagger in east.

Opening Exercises of Temple Rite.

Seated in the west, facing east, read:

The spinning ball of the earth in her annual dance around her Lord the Sun enters Aries. He in stately stride leaves the summer signs and enters the Sign of Libra. This is the Autumnal Equinox when day equals night. The time of reaping, ingathering and harvest is at hand, a time of thanksgiving and rejoicing. Let all the earth adore the Lord of the Universe.

Stand. Raise both arms in adoration and pray:

Holy art thou, Lord of the Universe!
Holy art Thou, whom nature hath not formed.
Holy art Thou, the vast and the mighty One.
Lord of the light and of the darkness!

Kneel or prostrate yourself and humbly give thanks for all personal blessings received. Then rise and dance with joy deosil around Altar singing a song of thanksgiving and praise. Finish dance in the west, sit and contemplate the many joys that are yours. Perhaps a reading or recitation of St. Francis' "Canticle of the Sun".

Rise and circumambulate deosil to the south. Take up Rod, hold it high with male end upward and proclaim:

By the power of Yah, the Yode of Tetragrammaton and the Wand of Will abrogated is the Password used during the Ascending Signs. The Password for the next six months shall be . . . . . In the name of the wisdom, the joy, the justice and the infinite mercy of the One Eternal Spirit.

With male tip of Rod touch the Ace of Wands, whispering:

Root of the Powers of Fire! The new Password is . . . . . So inform the Lords.

Go to west. With female end of Rod touch the Ace of Cups and whisper:

Root of the Powers of Water! The new Password is . . . . . So inform the Ladies.

Circumambulate to east. With male tip of Rod touch the Ace of Swords, whisper:

Root of the Powers of Air! The new Password is . . . . . So inform the Masters.

Go deosil to north. With female end of Rod touch the Ace of Pentacles, whisper:

Root of the Powers of Earth! The new Password is . . . . . So inform the Maidens.

Go to east, face Altar, balance the Rod by holding it horizontally with both hands, sayings:

Now is the time that night equals day and day equals night. The one balances the other and equilibrium is attained. The entire secret of the occult lies in the knowledge of equilibrium. But before equilibrium can be attained, balance must be maintained. I seek to maintain balance of the four essences of my being so as to attain equilibrium and thereby find the quintessence, the stone of the wise, the summmum bonum, true wisdom and perfect haypiness. So I pledge myself and so mote it be!

Continue to south, replace Rod. Go to west, take up Cup with cider, offer it, spill a little among the foliage in center of Altar and say:

I offer the juice of autumn fruit to the Great Ones beyond and behind my being in devotion and in gratitude. May they bless this oblation to my service and me to theirs.

Drink the cider, replace Cup. Pause in contemplation. Return to seat. Perform Closing Exercises of Temple Rite.

Autumnal Feast

Near the time of the Fall Equinox have a feast, a dance, a party, to which invite family and/or friends, both those still in the physical and those in other dimensions. Eat, drink and be merry! Have fun, tell stories, play music and games. make love, rejoice with an exceeding great rejoicing! If circumstances prevent a large gathering of people, have a small gathering. If even this is impossible, then invite discarnate entities, elemental spirits or even non-human physical beings, but have a feast anyway!

FESTIVAL OF THE WINTER SOLSTICE

"Deck the halls with boughs of holly,
Tra-la-la-la-la, tra-la-la-la!
Tis the season to be jolly,
Tra-la-la-la-la, tra-la-la-la."

The traditional Christmas Tree or branches of spruce or pine, pine cones, holly, mistletoe, bright red ribbon, red candles, green bayberry candles, gold ornaments, frankincense, myrrh, fruit, nuts, candy, spiced drinks—are all paraphanalia of the Festival of the Winter Solstice, celebrating the annual birth of the Sun. The giving of alms to the poor and of gifts to family and friends, especially children, feasting, singing, dancing, merry-making in general—mark the Yuletide a time of love and good will, and, as such, is entered into joyfully and enthusiastically by the Theurgist.

Temple Rite of the Winter Solstice

In the magical sense, midnight is halfway between sunset and sunrise. Just before magical midnight when the Sun is nearest to $0°$ Capricorn, either before or after, is the proper time of this rite.

On the Altar is one tall unlighted red candle in the center of a wreath of evergreen with pine cones and holly. The four Magical instruments are in their proper places on the Altar, the Cup is empty. On side tables are a cigarette lighter or matches with ashtray, the Censer with charcoal, and frankincense and myrrh in south; a pitcher of spiced wine (previously boil allspice and sugar in water and add small amount to warmed red wine along with whole cloves and cinnamon stick) in west; a piece of fruitcake on a plate in the north; and gold (golden Christmas Tree balls in a green glass bowl, for instance) with a gift to the Temple (a new Altar-cloth, a thurible, or whatever might enhance or be needed in your private Temple working) and gifts for any others who are to take part in the rite, in the east. Ritual Book on stand by chair in the west.

Either sky-clad or robed, girded and sandaled, enter Temple and salute Altar. If others are to take part, they follow the Theurgist in, salute the Altar and sit in the west. Silently light the candle in the center of the Altar and ignite the charcoal in the Censer in the south. Circumambulate deosil to west, face Altar, raise both arms in adoration (others stand) and pray:

Holy art Thou, Lord of the Universe!
Holy art Thou, whom Nature hath not formed.
Holy art Thou, the vast and the mighty One.
Lord of the light and of the darkness!

IAO! IAO! IAO! (Others repeat.)

Perform the Quabalistic Cross and the Sign of the Enterer. Sit. Enter the Silence. (Others follow suit,) After a while, take up Ritual Book and read:

At the time of the Autumnal Equinox our Lord the Sun left our hemisphere to take his light and his life to his children on the other side of the equator. We rejoice for them, our bretheren of the south latitudes. But for us his light has decreased, his heat has lessened. And so it seems that our Lord the Sun has grown weak and old— is dying. The cold winds blow from out of the north, our bones are chilled. Nature shrouds herself in a mantle of snow. All is still and quiet, as we are wont to be in the presence of death.

Pause. Arise, go to north of Altar. Contemplate the candle flame for a minute, then suddenly blow it out. Say:

The king is dead! Long live the king!
(Response: The king is dead! Long live the king!)

All lights in the room are extinguished with the candle flame. Slowly grope through the darkness via the east to the south, saying:

The people that walk in darkness shall see a great light; they that dwell in the land of the shadow of death, upon them shall the light shine.

Find and light the cigarette lighter or a match, saying:

For unto us a child is born, unto us a son is given.

(Response: A child is born! A son is given!)

Re-light the candle in the center of the Altar and say:

And his name shall be called Wonderful.

(Response: Wonderful!)

Counsellor.

(Response: Counsellor!)

The Mighty God.

(Response: Mighty! Mighty! Mighty!)

The Prince of Peace.

(Response: Peace! Peace! Peace!)

51

Circumambulate deosil to east. Read:

> Listen to his words: "I am the Ancient Child. I am Yesterday, To-day and Tomorrow. My name is Alpha and Omega, the Beginning and the End. Under the glittering horns of Capricornus when the mountains of the north glistened like the teeth of the black wolf in the cold light of the Moon did Miriam seek the cave below the cavern, in which no light had ever shone, to bring forth the Light of the World. And on the third day she departed from the cave and entering the Stable of the Sun she placed her child in the Manger of the Moon. Likewise was Mithras born under the tail of the Sea-Goat, and Horus and Krishna—all mystic names of the Child of Light. My dwelling house is built betwixt the water and the earth; the pillars thereof are of fire, and the walls are of air, and the roof above is the breath of my nostrils which is the spirit of the life of man. I am born as an egg in the east, of silver and gold and opalescent with the colors of precious stones, and with my glory is the breast of the horizon made purple and scarlet and orange and green, many-colored as a great peacock caught up in the coils of a serpent of fire. Lo! I am as a babe born in a crib of lilies and roses and wrapped in the swaddling bands of June. Mine hands are delicate and small and my feet are shod in flame so that they touch not the kingdoms of this earth. I arise and leave the cradle of my birth and wander through the valleys and over the hills across the sun-scorched deserts of day and through the cool groves of night. Everywhere, everywhere, I find myself in the deep pools and in the dancing streams and in the many-colored surface of the mere, there I am white and wonderful, a child of loveliness and of beauty, a child to entice songs from the wild rose and kisses from the zephyrs of dawn."

Go by south to west. Prostrate yourself or kneel before the Altar. (Others kneel.) Say:

> Thee I (we) adore, O hidden splendor, Thee,
> Who in the Flame dost design to be;
> I (we) worship Thee beneath this earthly veil,
> And here thy presence I (we) devoutly hail.

Adore in silence. Then arise (others stand) and begin deosil dance around Altar, singing:

> Joy to the world! The Lord is come;
> Let earth receive her king;
> Let ev'ry heart prepare him room,
> And heav'n and nature sing,
> And heav'n and nature sing,
> And heav'n, and heav'n and nature sing.

(Beckon others into the dance.)

> Joy to the earth! Her prince is born;
> Let men their songs employ;
> While fields and floods, rocks, hills and plains.
> Repeat the sounding joy,
> Repeat the sounding joy,
> Repeat, repeat the sounding joy.
>
> He rules the world with love and grace,
> And makes the nations prove

The glories of his righteousness
And wonders of his love,
And wonders of his love,
And wonders, and wonders of his love.

After the dance (and the others are seated), go the south, take up frankincense and myrrh, and say:

The Magi greeted the Avatar of the Piscean Age with gifts of frankincense and myrrh. I (we) joyfully follow their august example.

Cast the incense onto the glowing charcoal. Cense the Altar, saying:

May my life (our lives) be as a sweet fragrance in the nostril of the Lord of the Aeon!

Replace Censer. Go to west. Take pitcher of wine, pour some into the Cup, saying:

Blessed be the womb that bringeth forth the Light of the World!

Replace pitcher. Elevate Cup with both hands, saying:

The warm life blood of the Lord of the Ages!

Replace Cup on Altar. Go to north, take plate with fruit-cake, elevate it, saying:

Mother Earth.

Put plate with cake next to Cup. Take Rod and make Circled Cross over the cake and wine, saying:

Blessed be this oblation. In the name of the wisdom, the joy, the justice and the infinite mercy of the One Eternal Spirit. Amen.

(Response: Amen.)

Eat the cake. Drink the wine. (If others are present, the plate and wine are to be passed around deosil.)

Go to east. Take gold, offer it, saying:

They presented unto him a gift of gold.

Put your gift upon the Altar, saying:

I place my gift upon the Altar of Beth-El.

(If others have gifts for the Temple, they do and say the same. If there are gifts for others present, they are now distributed with the greeting:
Blessed be!)

Return to south. Read:

The Sun has reached the nadir of his southern trek, thus symbolically has died. But in entering Capricorn he is born anew. This is the Winter Solstice, the first day of winter. Winter! The snugness of wild life housed in tiny fur-lined baskets of grass. The fairy writing on fresh snow-fall by many tiny scampering feet. The blueness of the winter sky and the darting streaming pennants of the northern lights. A time of short days and long nights. A time of frost and snow, of chill winds and waiting earth. A time of sleep and rest. I (let us) approach the gates of winter!
O thou Source of Light and Life whose scattered seeds we are on

earth and in whom all endings are but new beginnings of another period of life, be thou close to me (us) who wait before the gates of winter. May my (our) Holy Guardian Angel help me (us) to realize the long night and death of winter leads to the dawn and resurrection of spring! May the welcome warmth of thy eternal love envelop and protect me (us).

(Response: Amen.)

Return to west. Sit. Enter the Silence. Perform the Quabalistic Cross. Then say HUA! while rising and at the same time shoving hands upward, outward and downward as a diver coming up out of water. Give the Sign of Silence.

Naturally, all of this calls for a party afterward!

FUNERAL RITES OF THEURGY

Theurgic Funeral Service

Our help is in the Name of the Lord who made heaven and earth. Eheieh (ay-HEE-yuh), Yahweh, Elohim, El, Elohim Gebor, Tetragrammaton Aloah Va Daath (ah-LOW-ah vah dah-AHTH), Yahweh Tzabaoth (za-BAH-oth), Elohim Tzabaoth, Shaddai El Chai, Adonai Malekh (MAH-lek). The Lord is nigh unto all them that call upon him, to all that call upon him in truth.

Lord, thou hast been our dwelling place in all generations. Before the mountains were brought forth, or ever thou hadst formed the earth and the world, even from everlasting to everlasting, thou art God.

Holy art Thou, Lord of the Universe!
Holy art Thou, whom nature hath not formed.
Holy art Thou, the vast and the mighty One.
Lord of the light and of the darkness.

Thine (touch forehead) is the kingdom (touch chest) and the power (touch right shoulder) and the glory (touch left shoulder) forever and ever (open hands together pointing up, head bowed). Amen.

Dear friends, we are met together to celebrate the passing into a higher life our dear brother (sister) _____ It is but natural that we who have known and loved him (her) should regret his (her) departure from amongst us, yet on this occasion it is our duty to think not of ourselves, but of him (her). Therefore must we endeavor to lay aside the thought of our personal loss and dwell only upon his (her) great (and most glorious) gain.

Let us remember that this life is but a training for the life to come, and when each has accomplished his work on earth he is called to continue that work in a higher sphere As you think how blessed is your loved one who has gone from the limitations of space and time of this physical plane into the spacelessness and timelessness of the Immeasurable Regions, it gives you joy rather than sorrow. And since the Astral, Mental and Spiritual planes interpenetrate this our physical world, your loved one can often be so very, very near, whenever he (she) chooses, for he (she) is not dead but sleepeth for a while, and when awakened can become once again a companion and a comfort.

> I cannot say, and I will not say
> That he (she) is dead. He (she) is just away.
>
> With a cheery smile and a wave of the hand,
> He (she) has wandered into the little-known land.
>
> And left us dreaming how very fair
> It needs must be since he (she) lingers there.
>
> And you who with the wildest yearn
> For the old-time step and the glad return,
>
> Think of him (her) as faring on, as dear
> In the love of there as the love of here;
>
> Think of him (her) still as the same, I say,
> For he (she) is not dead—he (she) is just away.

Let us pray:

O thou Single Source of Light and Life whose scattered seeds we are on earth, thou art the Lord of Life, and Conqueror over Death. Thou art our refuge and strength, a very present help in trouble. Breathe thy peace into our hearts and remove from us all fear of death. Help us to perceive that we are spiritual beings living in a spiritual universe, and that while the things that are seen with physical eyes are temporal and pass away, the spiritual things which we now glimpse but dimly are real and eternal. And give to us a blessed sense of that eternal love that holds us all. Comfort us who mourn, and give us grace, in the presence of death, to worship thee, the everlasting and eternal God. Amen.

> The Lord is my shepherd; I shall not want.
> He maketh me to lie down in green pastures:
> He leadeth me beside the still waters.
> He restoreth my soul:
> He leadeth me in the paths of righteousness for his name's sake.
> Yea, though I walk through the valley of the shadow of death,
> I will fear no evil: for thou art with me;
> Thy rod and thy staff they comfort me.
> Thou preparest a table before me in the presence of mine enemies:
> Thou anointest my head with oil;
> My cup runneth over.
> Surely goodness and mercy shall follow me all the days of my life:
> And I will dwell in the house of the Lord forever.

> There is no death! The stars go down
> To rise upon some other shore;
> And bright in heaven's jeweled crown
> They shine forevermore.
>
> There is no death! The dust we tread
> Shall change beneath the summer showers
> To golden grain, or mellow fruit,
> Or rainbow-tinted flowers.
>
> There is no death! An angel form
> Walks o'er the earth with silent tread;
> He bears our best loved ones away,
> And then we call them "dead."

Born unto that undying life,
They leave us but to come again;
With joy we welcome them—the same
Except in flesh and pain.

And ever near us, though unseen,
The dear immortal spirits tread;
For all the boundless universe
Is life—there are no dead.

(Obituary, if one be desired.)

(Address, if one be desired. Even so, let it be short.)

Let us pray:

O Lord, thou hast dominion over all souls everywhere and dost hold all thy creation in the everlasting arms of thy love. We pray thee for the peace and progression of thy servant . . . . , that he (she) ever living unto thee, may find in thy continued and unceasing service the perfect consummation of joy.

Peace in the eternal grant unto him (her) O Lord.
And let light perpetual shine upon him (her).
Come forth to meet him (her) ye Angels of the Lord!
Receive him (her) unto your fellowship, O ye Saints, Masters, Adepts.
May the Choirs of Angels receive him (her).
And guide him (her) into the brightness of the everlasting light. Amen.

Likewise, O Lord, we pray thee for those who love thy servant, those whom thou hast called to sacrifice the joy of his (her) earthly presence. Do thou, O Lord, comfort them with the balm of thy loving kindness, that, strengthened by thee and resting upon the surety of thy wisdom, they may put aside their thoughts of sorrow and grief, and pour upon him (her) only such thoughts of love as may help him (her) in the higher life to which thou hast now called him (her). Amen.

The Lord bless you and keep you. The Lord make his face to shine upon you, and be gracious unto you. The Lord lift up his countenance upon you, and give you peace. Amen.

The Committal Service

At the grave, the body (or ashes) having been lowered, the officiant shall say:

Forasmuch as it hath pleased Almighty God to call to higher dimensions our brother (sister) hence departed, we therefore commit his (her)

(a.) cast-off body to the ground, earth to earth,

(b.) ashes to their resting place,

(Here some earth is cast upon the coffin or container by the Officiant or someone standing by.)

ashes to ashes, dust to dust, that in that more glorious astral body which he (she) now weareth, he (she) may be free from earthly chains to serve God as he (she) ought.

56

For I say unto you: God created man to be immortal and made him to be an image of God's own eternity. In God's care rests this our loved one, whom the Lord hath designed to draw nearer to the vision of the Eternal Beauty. Ever praising God therefore, let us in firm but humble confidence call upon him and say:

O Father of Light and Life, we pray to thee to fill our hearts with calm and peace and to open within us the eyes of the soul, that we may see the radiance and glory that thou art pouring upon us. In thy limitless love thou wilt make allowance for our human love as we pray thee to grant eternal peace and progression unto this our dear brother (sister), and that light perpetual may shine upon him (her). May he (she) with us all in due time cross the Abyss and attain unto the Understanding, the Wisdom and the Crown of the glorious Supernal Triad. And so mote it be.

Now may awareness of the gracious motherhood of Binah (BEE-nuh), the potent fatherhood of Chokmah (HOKE-muh) and the shining Crown of Kether be with us all evermore. Amen.

Private Temple Rite for
One Whose Death Was Sudden or Violent

On Altar is an object-link with the deceased such as a personal belonging, a signature, a photograph, the Tarot Court card most descriptive, or the full name written on virgin parchment or white paper. Also on the Altar is a tall white candle in a holder, the four Instruments in their proper places with water and a sprig of hyssop or mint in the Cup, and, if desired, a bouquet of flowers. Censer with charcoal and Frankincense and lighter or matches on stand in south. Ritual Book on stand by chair in west.

Perform Opening Exercises of Temple Rite, igniting the charcoal after lighting the candle.

Seated in the west, whisper:

All-loving and heavenly Father, look down upon me (us) in my (our) grief for one taken so suddenly from us in the midst of physical life, and strengthen me (us) that I (we) may have courage and confidence in thine unfailing mercy. Amen.

After a while, stand, go by north to east, face Altar. Touch lovingly the object-link and visualize the deceased standing in the west, facing you. Call aloud three times his or her full name and say:

The shock of sudden death is yours. The silver cord that bound you to your physical body has broken. That physical body is dead. But **you** are not dead. You are alive in your astral body, your soul body. Perhaps you are confused, distraught, even fearful. I offer you my aid. Come, let us worship together.

Take object-link into left hand, press it to your breast. Repeat deceased's full name and say:

Our help is in the Name of the Lord who made heaven and earth. Eheieh, Yahweh, Elohim, El, Elohim Gebor, Tetragrammaton Aloah Va Daath, Yahweh Tzabaoth, Elohim Tzabaoth, Shaddai El Chai,

Adonai Malekh. The Lord is nigh unto all them that call upon him, to all that call upon him in truth. He will fulfill the desire of them that fear him; he also will hear them cry, and will save them. (Say again the full name of the deceased.) The Lord is thy light and thy salvation, whom shall you fear? The Lord is the strength of your life, of whom shall you be afraid? Though an host should encamp against you, your heart shall not fear. I had fainted unless I had believed to see the goodness of the Lord in the land of the everliving. Wait (first name of the deceased) upon the Lord, be of good courage, and he shall strengthen thy heart. Wait, I say, upon the Lord.

Replace object-link upon the Altar. Kneel and say:

In the name of (full name of deceased) I pray.

Almighty and most merciful Father, I have erred, and strayed from thy ways like a lost sheep. I have followed too much the devises and desires of my own heart. I have offended against thy holy laws. I have left undone those things which I ought to have done; and I have done those things which I ought not to have done. I have transgressed exceedingly in thought, word and deed (here strike the breast three times) through my fault, through my fault, through my most grievous fault. O Lord, have mercy upon me. Have mercy upon me, O Lord, according to thy great mercy. And according to the multitude of thy tender mercies, blot out my transgression. Wash me throughly from mine iniquity and cleanse me from my sin. Thou shalt purify me with hyssop and I shall be cleansed. Thou shalt wash me and I shall be made whiter than snow. Restore unto me the joy of thy salvation and strengthen me with a willing spirit. The sacrifice of God is an afflicted spirit; a contrite and humble heart, O God, thou wilt not despise.

Remain on knees in silence for a moment. Then stand and go to south Cast Frankincense onto the glowing charcoal, saying:

May the prayer in the name of (full name of the deceased) ascend to the Mercy Seat of God.

Cense the Altar and say:

(Name of deceased) I consecrate you with fire.

Replace Censer. Go to west. Dip fingers into Cup and sprinkle a few drops of water upon the object-link, saying:

(Name of deceased) I purify you with water.

Continue by north to east, face Altar. Make Circled Cross over object-link with Rod, saying:

(Name of deceased) the Lord, bless, preserve and sanctify you; the Lord in his loving kindness look down upon you and be gracious unto you; the Lord absolve you from all your sins and grant you the grace and comfort of the Holy Spirit. Amen.

Replace Rod. Walk slowly to the west, saying:

Lord, now suffer thou thy servant to depart in peace, that he (she) may enter into thy joy.

In west, make Circled Cross with right forefinger over the place where the deceased had been visualized as standing and say:

Depart in peace, beloved friend. Blessed be!

Sit. Perform Closing Exercises of Temple Rite.

THE RITUALS OF THE PENTAGRAM

Lesser Ritual of the Pentagram

Facing east, perform the Quabalistic Cross.

Right arm stretched straight before you, forefinger pointing, other fingers clasped to palm by thumb, draw a large five-pointed star in the air, visualizing the lines of the star as fire. Draw the pentagram by connecting the periods of the diagram below from one to six:

```
        1 . 6

   3 .          . 4

   5 .          . 2
```

Say the Deity Name: IHVH (Spell it Yod, He, Vau, He, or pronounce it Yahweh).

Turn right to south, draw the star in fire, say the Deity Name: ADNI (Adonai, ah-doh-NOE-ee).

Turn right to west, draw the star in fire, say the Deity Name: AHIH (Eheieh, ay-HEE-yuh).

Turn right to north, draw the star in fire, say the Diety Name: AGLA (AH-glah).

Turn right to face east again. Extending the arms on either side so as to make your body a cross, say:

> Before me Raphael;
> Behind me Gabriel;
> On my right hand, Michael;
> On my left hand, Auriel;
> For about me flames the Pentagram,
> And in the column stands the six-rayed Star.

Repeat the Quabalistic Cross

Greater Ritual of the Pentagram

The Pentagrams are traced in the air with the proper finger or appropriate instrument, the Name spoken aloud and the Sign given as below:

The Pentagrams of Spirit (or Aether)

Thumb extended and pointing forward, fingers clasped to palm.

59

Invoking		Banishing	
5 .		3 .	
2 .	. 3	1 . 6	. 5
4 .	1 . 6	4 .	. 2

Name: AHIH (Eheieh).

Sign: The Signs of the Portal are two. (1.) Invoking. Extend the hands together in front of you, back of hands touching, palms outward, separate them as if in the act of rendering asunder a veil or separating or opening curtains, then let hands fall to side. (2.) Banishing. Extend the hands wide apart in front of you, palms inward, bring them together as if closing the veil, then let hands fall to sides.

The Pentagrams of Fire

Forefinger or Rod.

Invoking		Banishing	
1 . 6		. 2	
3 .	. 4	5 .	. 4
5 .	. 2	3 .	1 . 6

Name: AL (El).

Sign: Raise both hands to forehead, palms out, thumbs along line of eyebrows, their tips touching, forefinger tips touching points upward, thus formulating the triangle of fire.

The Pentagrams of Water

Third or ring finger or Cup.

Invoking		Banishing	
4 .		. 4	
1 . 6	. 2	2 .	1 . 6
3 .	. 5	5 .	. 3

Name: ALHIM (Elohim).

Sign: Raise the arms to the sides until the elbows are almost on a level with the shoulders, bring the hands across the chest, touching the tips of the thumbs and the downward pointing forefingers so as to form a triangle apex downwards.

The Pentagrams of Air

Little finger or Dagger.

Invoking			Banishing	
4.				.4
2.	1.6		1.6	.2
5.	.3		3.	.5

Name: IHVH (Yahweh).

Sign: Stretch both arms upwards and outwards, the elbows bent at right angles, hands bent backward, palms upwards, as if supporting a weight.

The Pentagrams of Earth

Middle finger or Disk.

Invoking			Banishing	
1.6				.2
4.	.3		4.	.5
2.	.5		1.6	.3

Name: ADNI (Adonai).

Sign: Advance the right foot, stretch out the right hand upward and forward, the left hand downward and backward, palms open.

THE L. V. X. SIGNS

Facing east, stand upright, feet together, left arm at side, right forearm across body at diaphragm. Say:

I. N. R. I.
Yod, Nun, Resh, Yod.
Virgo, Isis, Mighty Mother.
Scorpio, Apophis, Destroyer.
Sol, Osiris, Slain and Risen.
Isis, Apophis, Osiris, IAO.

Extend the arms to either side so as to make your body a cross. Say:

The Sign of Osiris Slain.

Raise the right arm to point upward, keeping the elbow square, lower the left arm to point downward, keeping the elbow square, while turning the head over the left shoulder looking down so that the eyes follow the left forearm. Say:

The Sign of the Mourning of Isis.

Raise the arms at an angle of sixty degrees to each other above the head which is thrown back, and say:

The Sign of Apophis and Typhon.

Cross the arms on the breast so that the extended fingers almost touch the opposite shoulder, bow the head, and say:

The Sign of Osiris Risen.

Extend the arms again as in Sign of Osiris Slain and cross them again as in Sign of Osiris Risen, saying:

L.V.X., Lux, the Light of the Cross.

THE RITUALS OF THE HEXAGRAM

Lesser Ritual of the Hexagram

Perform the L.V.X. Signs.

The Hexagrams consist of two equilateral triangles. They are to be drawn and visualized as fire in the air as were the stars in the Lesser Ritual of the Pentagram. Make the triangle 1-2-3-4 first, then the a-b-c-d triangle.

Trace the Hexagram of the Air in the east, saying:

Ararita.

(Note: The word Ararita consists of the initials of a sentence in Hebrew which means, "One is His beginning; One is His individuality; His permutation is One.")

1 . 4

3 . b   c . 2

a . d

(In this Hexagram the bases of the two triangles coincide, forming a diamond.)

Turn right to face south. Trace the Hexagram of Fire in the south saying:

Ararita.

```
                    1 . 4

                    a . d

            3 .          . 2

            c .          . b
```

(This Hexagram consists of two triangles, both apices pointing upward. The top of the lower triangle should coincide with the central point of the upper one.)

Turn to face west. Trace the Hexagram of Water in the west, saying: Ararita.

```
            b .               . c

                  a 1 . 4 d

            3 .              . 2
```

(This Hexagram has the lower triangle placed above the upper so that their apices coincide.)

Turn to face north. Trace the Hexagram of Earth in the north, saying:

Ararita.

```
                    1 . 4

            b .           . c

            3 .           . 2

                    a . d
```

(This Hexagram forms the six-pointed Star of David It has the apex of the lower triangle pointing downward and the whole should be capable of inscription in a circle.)

Repeat the L.V.X. Signs.

The Banishing Ritual is identical, save that the direction of the lines of the two triangles must be reversed, going from 4 to 1, then D to A.

Greater Ritual of the Hexagram

To invoke or banish influence of Planets or Zodiacal Signs.

Perform the Lesser Ritual of the Hexagram, omitting the final L.V.X. Signs.

Then repeat the Hexagram of Earth and in its center draw the astrological symbol of the Planet or Sign you are dealing with, naming it three times.

Conclude with the L.V.X. Signs.

Success in invoking is known by a feeling of power or holiness, success in banishing by a feeling of cleanliness or freshness.

EXORCISM

Of Things

Method A. Make widdershins (counter-clockwise) circle over or around object with Rod or forefinger, saying:

By the power of Yah, the Yod of Tetragrammaton and the Wand of Will I exorcise and free from any and all contamination this . . . (name the object). Hekas! Hekas! Este Bibeloi! Be far from here, O ye profane!

Method B. Wash the object in running water or pour water over it, saying:

Great Mother! Great Mother! Great Mother of all! Give heed, dear Mother, give heed as I call! By the holy name Elohim may the waters of Binah (BEE-nuh) wash this . . . . . (name the object) . . . clean of all contamination. Be clean (good, dear, useful) . . . . . (name the object) . . . be clean.

Method C. Ignite flame while repeating the verse from Opening Exercises of Temple Rite beginning "From fire above to fire below", etc. Then pass the object quickly through the flame, saying:

May the holy fire of Michael burn away all dross and contamination from this . . . . . (name the object). Fire bright, fire keen, give light, make clean!

Method D. Hold object high in blowing wind, saying:

Blow, blow, brother wind! Take away all evil from this . . . . . (name the object). Sail away, dirt! ride the wind home!

Method E. Bury the object on a Friday just before sundown, and say:

May Mother Earth absorb and transmute all energies of this . . . . . (name the object) . . . cleansing it, renewing it, Earth to earth, ashes to ashes, dust to dust.

Early on the following Sunday morning dig up the object, saying:

It was sown in corruption, it is raised in incorruption; it was sown in dishonor, it is raised in glory; it was sown in weakness; it is raised in power. Thanks be to Mother Earth.

Method F. Christian Exorcism:

I exorcise thee, creature of . . . . (name the object) . . . by the living God (make Sign of the Cross with hand up to down, left to right, over the object) by the holy God (Sign of the Cross) by the omnipotent God (Sign of the Cross) that thou mayest be purified from all evil influence, in the name of him who is Lord of Angels and of men, who filleth the whole earth with his majesty and glory. Amen.

Method G. From the Greater Ritual of the Pentagram, make the Sign of Earth and draw the banishing Pentagram of Earth before the object, saying:

In the Name of Adonai, banished be all evil from this . . . . . (name the object). Hekas! Hekas! Este Bibeloi!

Of Places

Standing as near as possible in the exact center of the place, perform the Lesser Ritual of the Pentagram. Then, from the Greater Ritual of the Pentagram give the Signs of Fire, Water, Air, Earth and trace the banishing Pentagrams toward south, west, east and north, saying:

> In the Name of (El, Elohim, Yahweh, Adonai) I exorcise and banish all evil and contamination from this place. Hekas! Hekas! Este Bibeloi!

Next, trace the banishing Pentagram of Spirit directing it toward the ground or floor below you, saying: "In the Name of Eheieh" etc. and give the Sign of the Closing of Portal downward.

Then trace the invoking Pentagram of Spirit above you and give the Sign of the Opening of the Portal directed upward, saying:

> In the Name of Eheieh I invoke and welcome to this place any and all that is good, any and all that is true, any and all that is beautiful.

Finally make a Circled Cross over the spot where you were standing during the above and say:

> Blessed be this place and all who enter herein.
> So mote it be, so mote it be.

Of Hauntings

"Hauntings" are abnormal or unusual phenomena of a psychically caused nature (but often with physical effects) generally considered to be evil or at least disturbing to those witnessing or affected by them. They are associated primarily with places but also occasionally with families (some of the royalty of Europe and certain Irish family "banshees") and even rarely with individuals. They occur either regularly at definite times or intervals (anniversaries, full Moon, dark of the Moon, etc.) or spasmodically at irregular times and intervals seemingly without rhyme or reason, or they may be "once-occuring" but usually for a period of time varying from a few days to many years.

They are caused by (1.) thought-forms created usually under great emotional stress; (2.) earthbound spirits, discarnate human beings who usually have died under distressful circumstances and/or are seemingly held to a particular place because of some abnormal or unusual circumstances such as greatly exaggerated love of a place or of physical things (the miser's love for his hoarded money) or extraordinary feelings of hate, lust, revenge, fear, guilt, etc.; (3.) "poltergeists", prank-playing or mischeviousness such as furniture dancing around room, breaking of windows, dishes, etc., articles flying through the air catapulted by unseen hands, etc., which are thought forms (motivated) or thoughtless energy forms (unmotivated other than causing havoc) of a boy (rarely) or of a girl (usually) during time of puberty and before the sex-force is directed toward and expressed through sexual activity; or (4.) non-human astral entities such as nature-spirits.

To exorcise a haunting (or to "lay the ghost") it is necessary to first ascertain the type (1 to 4 above). This is done by a careful study and analysis of the phenomena, preferably by personal first-hand experience, otherwise of reports by trustworthy witnesses, authenticated if possible. It is wise to consider the possibility of natural physical causes such as the settling or sinking of the foundation of an old house causing doors to swing open or shut and creating "groaning" noises, such as decaying organic matter causing phosphoresence, such as "a big joke" or a hoax perpetrated by pranksters, such as mice in the wainscotting causing "rustling" sounds, etc., and also the possibility that the reporter of the phenomena is either deliberately lying so as later to boast, "I made it all up so as to expose or discredit that Exorcist," or is consciously or even unconsciously fabricating in order to attract attention because he or she is highly imaginative and is "thrilled" by the possibility of a haunting and an exorcism.

After the type of the haunting is ascertained, it is necessary then to decide whether an exorcism is advisable and just what form it should take.

(1.) **Thought-Form Haunting.** This is the classic form of haunting familiar from popular ghost stories—a headless phantom, a weeping woman wraith, rattling of chains, stealthy footsteps on creaking stairs, sudden coldness, etc. The atmosphere and the physical substance of and in a place are highly charged by a great explosion of thought and emotional energy in an act of violence such as a murder or a suicide, usually preceded or accompanied by a prolonged period of intense suffering and/or extreme cruelty. The explosion of energy creates the thought-form which is composed of mental-astral-etheric substance. Thereafter, when stimulated and energized by timing or similar atmospheric or planetary vibrations, the thought-form becomes activated and the phenomena occur. These ghosts are not discarnate human beings, are not non-human astral entities, are not angels or demons; they are things which have been made. Since their cohesive substance is etheric and since etheric substance is returned most quickly to its free, unattached state by fire, the simplest way to get rid of them is to burn down the structure where the phenomena occur. This, of course, is, in by far the majority of cases, undesirable if not impossible.

Just before the Full Moon perform the Lesser Ritual of the Pentagram and follow immediately with the Greater Ritual of the Pentagram, using the banishing Pentagrams. In most cases this should suffice, but where the haunting is particularly strong the Greater Ritual of the Hexagram should be performed, using the banishing Hexagrams and banishing every Zodiacal Sign and every Planet.

(2.) **Haunting by Earthbound Spirits.** These discarnate human beings are. as a rule, miserably unhappy and in extreme states of fear, remorse, hatred. frustration, depression or other destructive emotion. Occasionally, however, they are placid, resigned, puzzled perhaps as to their condition but almost content even though very lonely. Some are quite content as long as they are undisturbed in the place, house or room or near the physical object they so dearly love, but become agitated, fearful, resentful, when their complacency is interrupted. Others either do not know they have died or stubbornly refuse to accept the fact of their death. The important thing to remember about these unfortunates is that they are human beings and should be treated as such. Some of the haunting phenomena they create are distress signals asking for help (knockings, rappings, flashes of light, etc.), and these spirits respond eagerly to proffers of aid. Other phenomena are created by the very presence of the discarnate entity (rustlings, sighings, groanings, etc.) who may not want any help and may even resent or refuse offers of aid.

A seance held where the haunting occurs, with a trance medium participating, would be a logical first step in dealing with this type of phenomena. One such ran something like this:

Three people including a medium sat at a table in the haunted room. They talked quietly for a while then repeated the Lord's Prayer and sang a hymn. The medium shuddered during the hymn then slumped in her chair with eyes closed. Suddenly she sat bolt upright, eyes still closed, pounded the table with a fist and spoke:

Medium: What the hell's going on here?

Sitter: We're here to help you. What's your name?

Medium: Henry Smith. What's yours?

Sitter: I'm John Jones and this is my wife, Mary. The lady you are talking through is Margo May.

Medium: Whatta-ya mean, talking through? I'm not talking through anyone. And what are you doing here, anyway? Who asked you? This is **my** place and I didn't invite you. Get out! Do you hear me? Get out!

Sitter: Oh, we're not going to stay. We have just come calling with the idea that perhaps we might pray with you.

Medium: Pray with me? Oh, I get it. You're some of those religious fanatics who go around giving out pamphlets and asking for contributions. Well, I'll make a donation. But I don't seem to have— I'm sorry, I'm a little confused—I must not be well—things have been a little mixed-up for me lately—

Sitter: Since you died. Did you commit suicide?

Medium: (Sobbing) I tried to. I just couldn't take it any longer. (Bitterly laughing) But I messed that up too, like everything else.

Sitter: You didn't mess it up. You succeeded.

Medium: Well, I'll be damned!

Sitter: You evidently are damned to stay here for awhile. But there's help for you—over there and here. Would you like to pray with us?

Medium: I'm dead? I really did it? But it can't be! I'm not dead! What are you talking about? I'm not dead—I'm here, aren't I?

Sitter: **You** are here, but your physical body is not. It is dead—you killed it. But **you** are a spirit and you are now in the spirit world even though you do not seem to be conscious of it. Do you understand me? (There was no response. A long pause.) Henry Smith! Are you here?

Medium: I heard mom calling me, but I thought I was delirious. She's been dead a long time.

Sitter: Now **you** call for **her**! She can help you or she can get help for you over there. Call your mother, Henry! O mother of Henry Smith, your son needs you!

The medium sank back into her chair and was utterly still for awhile. Then she stirred and awakened. The Private Temple Rite for One Whose Death was Sudden or Violent was then performed. Many weeks later a message through another psychic was received from an "H. S." of thanks for help given.

If no direct communication with the discarnate entity is possible, then a sensitive's psychic report, made in the place where the haunting occurs, should be obtained. If at all possible, the Private Temple Rite referred to above should be performed in the place. Later, the place should be exorcised by the rite of Exorcism of Places given previously.

(3.) **Poltergeist Haunting.** The child whose awakening sex-energy creates the phenomena should be identified and given psychological counseling during which any conscious or unconscious resentments, hostilities and fears should be gently probed and assuaged. An exciting or interesting visit elsewhere by the child would remove the sources of energy and the phenomena would either stop suddenly or would weaken and soon cease. In all cases poltergeist phenomena lasts only a few weeks at most. All such children have loosely-constructed etheric bodies and so could easily become excellent mediums. The house where the phenomena occur should be exorcised, but not with the child present.

(4.) **Haunting by Nature Spirits.** Sometimes a favorite spot of nature spirits is intruded upon by man in his endless encroachment upon nature. A new road is constructed and shortly thereafter a certain stretch of it becomes "accident prone" even though it was built according to all engineering safety standards and is exactly the same as many miles in both directions. Yet the number of accidents on that particular spot or area far exceed the average of any other given stretch of the road. Or a house is built on a particularly lovely secluded woodland spot. Even during its construction strange things begin to happen—tools disappear from one place and are found in another, things expertly made and handled by competent workmen just don't seem to fit and little important parts are missing—and after the family moves in, strange things continue to happen--the perfectly good furnace "acts up" frequently as does the water and electric supply even though the neighbors have no trouble at all with discolored or "funny tasting" water or flickering lights; the house "feels" uncomfortable and at times seems to actually tremble or gives viewers the appearance of being slightly askew; plants either wither and die or grow wildly; ants, moths roaches, mice invade the house, birds and insects "scold" it, etc.

As nearly as possible the original setting should be restored nearby even if smaller in extent. Trees, rocks, boulders, water, wild flowers, fern, fallen tree—whatever was in the original area should be included in the new setting. A naturally formed Cup such as a hollowed-out rock containing honey with a pinch of thyme and a few drops of blood or semen should be placed in the area to attract the elementals and the Greater Invoking Ritual of the Pentagram performed there. Afterward the new area should be "off-limits" to humans except for a rare visit by a sympathetic Theurgist or children of all ages. The original site can then be exorcised by the Lesser Ritual of the Pentagram followed by the Greater Banishing Ritual of the Pentagram.

Of Persons

To cleanse one's own aura: The Lesser Ritual of the Pentagram. After a particularly difficult bout with unbalanced forces: The Greater Banishing Ritual of the Pentagram.

Method A. Of another. Make widdershins circle before or over the person with Rod or forefinger saying:

68

By the power of Yah, the Yod of Tetragrammaton and the Wand of Will, I exorcise and free you from any and all contamination. Hekas! Hekas! Este Bibeloi! Be far from here, O ye profane!

Method B. Christian Exorcism:
I exorcise thee . . . . . (name) . . .by the living God (make Sign of the Cross before or over the person) by the holy God (Sign of Cross) by the omnipotent God (Sign of Cross) that thou mayest be purified from all evil influence, in the name of him who is Lord of Angels and of men, who filleth the whole earth with his majesty and glory. Amen.

Method C. Perform the Greater Banishing Ritual of the Pentagram before the person in this order: Earth, Air, Water, Fire, saying:

In the Name of (Adonai, Yahweh, Elohim, El) I exorcise and banish all evil and contamination from you. Hekas! Hekas! Este Bibeloi! (In cases of Possession or Obession, conclude with Spirit or Aether and say as above but with the Name of Eheieh.)

THEURGIC BLESSING

The simplest (and as effective as any) form of Theurgic Blessing is to make a Circled Cross up to down, right to left, then a clockwise circle beginning at the left, with forefinger or Rod, saying: Blessed be!

Christian Blessing

The Sign of the Cross is made with the straight up right hand, the hand open, fingers together and straight, thumb straight and in line with the hand, the palm of the hand facing left. The elbow is bent to approximately a forty-five degree angle, the hand bent backward at wrist, making the upward-pointing tips of the fingers to be about in line with the lips. A cross is then formed in the air with a downward movement of the arm, then a left to right movement, while saying:

In the Name of the Father, and of the Son, and of the Holy Ghost, Amen.

Esoteric Benediction

The right arm is extended forward and upward at an angle of approximately forty-five degrees. The thumb, forefinger and middle finger are extended and apart, the ring and little fingers are bent toward the palm. Say one of the following:

The Lord bless you and keep you. The Lord make his face to shine upon you and be gracious unto you. The Lord lift up his countenance upon you and give you peace.

Fulfill now thy promise unto us, our Father, and give unto us thy ministering angels to watch over us in all our ways. Amen.

Now the Lord of Peace himself give you peace always by all means. The Lord be with you all.

PORTFOLIO OF MAGIC

Dreaming True

When the Moon is approaching the Full, put a pinch (½ teaspoon) each of Lavender, Peppermint, Poppy Seed, Rosemary and Thyme in a sauce pan with three cups of water, bring to a boil, reduce heat and allow to simmer for three minutes. Strain and pour into your bath water. While bathing fumigate bedroom with incense you have composed by pounding in a mortar with a pestle one teaspoon each of Aloes, Camphor, Cucumber Seed, Jasmine and Sandalwood. Write a question on a piece of white paper, repeating it aloud three times, and put it with (not in) a sachet or small cloth bag containing Wormwood herb under your pillow. The question will be answered in a dream.

Yes or No Dream

Waxing Moon. On a slip of white paper write: WHITE is YES. BLACK is NO. In the center of the paper draw the symbols of the Moon, Mercury and Uranus, under which write a question so worded that the answer must be either yes or no, repeating aloud the question three times. Put the slip of paper with sachet of Wormwood under your pillow. During the next three nights you will dream. In the dream something white or black will be emphasized, answering the question. The content of the dream need not concern the question.

Ascertaining the Sex of An Unborn Child

Make a pendulum by inserting cotton thread through a ring of the pregnant female. Do not tie the thread but hold the two ends. Hold the pendulum over the abdomen of the prone mother-to-be, saying:

Watchman, watchman, what is our joy?
To the left a girl, to the right a boy.

Within a few minutes the ring will begin to swing, at first to-and-fro and then in a circle. A clockwise circle indicates male, counterclockwise is female.

Preparation of Love Philtres

Waxing Moon. On a Friday shortly after midnight, early morning, mid-afternoon or late evening.

On center of Altar is Tarot Atu III, the Empress, head eastward, flanked by the Two of Cups on her left and the Ten of Cups on her right. Dirctly below her is the Nine of Cups, the wish card, flanked by the two court cards representing the two people for whom the philtre is being made. Sweet-smelling flowers such as carnations, freesias, jasmine, lilac, narcissus, roses, are strewn among the cards or may form a wreath around them or may be in a low vase at the Empress' head. Green or pink candles may also be on the Altar if desired. Rod in south and Cup with water in west. On side table by the chair in the west are Ritual Book, mortar and pestle, and ingredients of the

Philtre. On side table in the south are lighter or matches with ashtray, Censer with charcoal and a container of incense which consists of any combination of the following: Aloes, Jasmine, Myrtle, Rosemary, Rose Petals, Sandalwood, Verbena, Violet Leaves or Blossoms, to which has been added a drop or two of Oil of Musk and/or blood and/or semen and/or dried white of egg.

Perform Opening Exercises of Temple Rite, igniting the charcoal at the time of lighting the candles and casting the incense upon the glowing charcoal and censing the Altar after giving the Sign of the Enterer. If possible, have record or tape of romantic music (whatever "turns you on") playing softly during the following:

Seated in the west, facing east, with eyes closed vividly recall memories of your own past loves and romantic attachments, re-living them with all the joy, tenderness, agony, passion of a great first love. Do this until you find yourself sighing, laughing, perhaps weeping. Then, gazing at the Empress, whisper:

O Goddess of Love and Lady of Delight! Great thou art and greatly to be honored! Thanks be to thee for these bittersweet memories of mine! Many names are yours—Isis, Hathor, Aphrodite, Venus, Lolita, Freya, Rhiannon, Habondia, Aradia— but by whatever name you are known you are indeed the Lady of Delight and Goddess of Love! In thy name do I proceed to this work of love.

Stand. Take the two court cards, put them face together, saying:

(Name of first person) love (name of second person). (Name of second person) love (name of first person).

Put the two cards face together on top of the Nine of Cups. On them put face upward the Two of Cups and the Ten of Cups, and say:

As the love of Osiris and Isis, of Orpheus and Eurydice, of Romeo and Juliet, of David and Jonathan, of Boaz and Ruth, of Damon and Pythias, of Sappho and her friend, of Yang and Yin, of red and blue, of the Rod and the Cup, so may be the love of (first names of the two people). True love has he (she), true love has she (he) true love, true love, so mote it be!

Then cast one of the following spells:

CORIANDER SPELL. Count seven Coriander seeds into the mortar, pound them well with the pestle while visualizing and naming three times the people concerned. Then say:

Warm seed, warm heart,
May they never be apart.

Cast the powder into the Cup, stir it with Rod, saying:

Blest be he (she) blest be she (he),
May their love a true love be.

Make Circled Cross over Cup. Allow the herb to steep for several hours then strain the philtre through cheesecloth and introduce it secretly into the food or drink of the person or persons the spell is desired to affect.

Perform Closing Exercises of Temple Rite, omitting the widdershins circumambulation.

MISTLETOE SPELL. Pound in mortar dried Mistletoe berries with dried Vervain leaves or Lovage and Thyme or Anise seeds, saying:

Mistletoe, dear Mistletoe,
Cause love to sprout, cause love to grow.

Say the names three times and proceed as in Coriander Spell.

PERIWINKLE SPELL. Same as above but with these ingredients: dried
Perwinkle leaves, Cinquefoil and Rose Petals, and these words:

A loving lad, a loving lass,
Periwinkle brings to pass.

—or—

As a loving lad loves a loving lass
So Periwinkle brings love to pass.

Note. Instead of love of a particular person for a particular person, it is
much wiser to work for love between a particular person and "an acceptable partner" which words are then substituted for the name of the second
party. The court card chosen for the acceptable partner should be comple-
mentary to the known court card, as Cups to Wands or Swords to Pentacles.
The first party saturates a handkerchief or a sachet with the philtre and
wears it. Or he or she may be anointed with the philtre on top of each foot,
on genitals, on palm of each hand, on lips and on heart, with these words:

I anoint you the sevenfold anointment of love. May your feet carry
and lead you to love. May your member consummate and fulfill love.
May your hands touch and serve love. May your lips speak and kiss
love. And may your heart give and receive love. Love as thou wilt I
say to thee; and as thou wilt, so mote it be!

Sachets of Love

The traditional witch sachet is a small bag or pocket, one to three inches
square, made of white cloth and sewn or tied with red thread, yarn or ribbon,
containing dried herbs, leaves, flowers, roots. The sachet is to be worn or
carried by the person desirous of attracting love and is often tucked under
the pillow at night. The ingredients are reduced to a powder by pounding in
a mortar with a pestle and consist of any combination of at least three of the
following: Aloes, Balm, Balm of Gilead Buds, Bergamot, Cowslip Flowers,
Jasmine Blossoms, Lavender, Lovage, Marigold, Marjoram, Mint, Myrtle,
Orris Root, Rosemary, Rose Petals, Sage, Sandalwood, Southernwood,
Thyme, Verbena Leaves, Vervain, Violet Blossoms or Leaves. The sachet
should be made on a Friday when the Moon is waxing, should be charged
with love and consecrated with such spoken words as:

May love within draw love without;
May lonely heart as fragrance blow
To draw sweet love from thereabout
So lonely heart may sweet love know!
Love, sweet love is here contained,
Love, sweet love out there is free;
May love without be here constrained
To love this lover—so mote it be!

Invocation of Kernunnos

Moon near or at Full. On a Thursday shortly after midnight, early morning, mid-afternoon or late evening.

On center of Altar is a statue or picture of Pan or a statue or picture of the Goat of Mendes or Tarot Atu XV, the Devil, head eastward, or a model of an erect penis or a picture of a naked man with an erect penis or any phallic symbol. Rod in south, Cup with red wine in west, Disk in north, Dagger in east. Scattered on Altar or formed in a wreath around the centerpiece are pine cones with fern, ivy, branches or twigs or leaves of evergreen such as pine, spruce, cedar, rhododendron or laurel, and any horns, teeth, hooves of hoofed animals that you can collect. Two red candles may also be on Altar, if desired. In side table in south are lighter or matches, Censer with charcoal, and a container of the incense which has been prepared by pounding in a mortar these ingredients: 2 parts Frankincense, 1 part Bay Leaves, 1 part Wormwood herb, 1 part Vervain herb, 1 part Patchouli Leaves. 1 part Cypress wood shavings or Pine needles, afterward adding a few drops of Oil of Musk, Oil of Cloves, Pine Oil (gum turpentine), Olive Oil, Honey, Red Wine and the operator's own semen or blood. On side table in east are equipment and/or ingredients for the spell to be cast. Ritual Book on side table by chair in west.

In preparing for the Ritual, after bathing, anoint the temples, the throat, the wrists and the feet with natural or synthetic Oil of Musk or Essence of Patchouli.

Perform Opening Exercises of Temple Rite, igniting the charcoal at the time of lighting the candles. If possible, have record or tape of music with a throbbing beat playing during the following.

Seated in the west, facing east, with eyes closed vividly imagine a passionate sexual experience or act and fantasize and feel it to the point of becoming sexually aroused. Then, gazing at the symbol on the Altar, whisper:

O Horned One! Magnificent you are and greatly to be praised! Your horn is erect and glad! As you are horned and horny (so may I be) (so may . . . . . be) (so may he whom I desire be).

Stand, circumambulate deosil to south, take incense, cast it into the Censer and cense Altar, saying:

(Censing left) Eko, Eko Azarak!
(Censing right) Eko, Eko Zomelak!
(Censing forward) Eko, Eko Kernunnos!

Replace Censer. Dance deosil around Altar, chanting:

Io Pan! Io Pan! Come over the sea
From Sicily and from Arcady!
Roaming as Bacchus, with fauns and pards
And nymphs and satyrs for thy guards!

Come with Artemis, silken shod,
And wash thy white thigh, beautiful god,
In the moon of the woods, on the marble mount,
The dimpled dawn of the amber fount!

Thrust the sword through the galling fetter,
All-devourer, all begetter;
Give me the sign of the Open Eye,
And the token erect of the thorny thigh.

I am Pan! Io Pan! Io Pan Pan! Pan!
I am thy mate, I am thy man,
Goat of thy flock, I am gold, I am god,
Flesh to thy bone, flower to thy rod.

With hoofs of steel I race on the rocks
Through solstice stubborn to equinox
And I rave, and I rape and I rip and I rend
Everlasting, world without end—

Manniken, maiden, maenad, man,
In the might of Pan.
Io Pan! Io Pan Pan! Pan! Io Pan!

Finish dance in the east, crouch there and visualize yourself in a small green clearing of a vast, dark forest. Hear in the distance a trampling and occasional cry of a wild beast as it crashes through the underbrush. Sense excitement in the air, even smelling it. Feel that something or someone, wildly exciting, is approaching you from behind. Do not look around but wait until you are conscious of a presence. Then whisper:

Pan! Bacchus! Phallic Hermes! Priapus!
Khem! Set! Horus! Arada! Kernunnos!
By whatever name and in whatever form you come,
You are the Generative Power! You are the Creative Force!
Privilege me to be your instrument!
Ordain me your priest (priestess)!

Energy will flow to, through, around and from you. Revel in this for awhile, then stand and say:

In thy name I cast this spell.

Perform one of the following:

INCREASING VIRILITY AND POTENCY IN ONE'S SELF. For the male Theurgist. Anoint and massage the crotch, scrotum, pubic hair and penis with Olive Oil which has been mixed with a few drops of at least three of the following: natural or synthetic oil, essence or extract of Ambergris, Cassia, Cedarwood, Civet, Cloves, Geranium, Jasmine, Musk, Patchouli, Pine, Rose, Vanilla. In doing so, say:

"Do what thou wilt" was said to me;
"Do what thou wilt" I say to thee!
Be strong, be powerful, and potent be—
Virility is thine! So mote it be!

Should ejaculation occur massage the semen back into the skin. Wash the hands afterward but not the body for at least eight hours. Perform the Closing Exercises of the Temple Rite omitting the widdershins circumambulation.

INCREASING VIRILITY AND POTENCY IN ANOTHER. Prepare same mixture as above, say the man's name three times and repeat the words above. Perform Closing Exercises of Temple, omitting widdershins circumambulation. Give the mixture to the man with instructions as above.

THE CINGULUM SPELL. Hairs from the head of the desired one. Three lengths of cord or twine. Sprinkle them with wine from the Cup and pass them through the incense smoke, saying:

74

With the power of Kernunnos and his potency
I charge you with vim, vigor and vitality.

Knot the ends of the twine and braid them together, binding the hair into the plait as you do so, saying:

Lord Kernunnos, I ask of thee,
Let ....(name) .... no pleasure,
sleep or solace see
Till heart and loins be turned to me!

Tie the free cord ends together in a knot and say:

And as I will, so mote it be!

Fasten the finished cord around the upper part of the thigh if you are a woman or around the genital organs if you are a man, tight enough not to slip, but not so tight as to restrict the circulation of the blood. Perform Closing Exercises of Temple Rite, omitting the widdershins circumambulation. Wear the cord until the next New Moon.

PLANETARY MAGIC SQUARES

Magic Squares, or Kameas, as they are often called, are arrangements of numbers so arranged as to yield the same number when added horizontally, vertically or diagonally. Also the sum of the total of all the numbers in the square is a number of special significance to which that square is referred.

Make the Magic Square by drawing with pen or pencil and ruler a large square and divide it by horizontal and vertical lines into the required number of boxes or smaller squares.

When the Magic Square is properly made and ceremonially charged and consecrated, it becomes a magnet to draw, a battery to hold, and a focus to express the particular energy of the luminary or planet.

The Sun gives life, authority, power, dignity, prominence, success in government and management.

The Moon gives contact with inner dimensions, dreams, change, travel, success with the public in general and women and children in particular.

Mercury gives magical power, ingenuity, know-how, duality, cleverness, success in communication, education, trade and travel.

Venus gives love, graciousness, beauty, success in romance and the arts.

Mars gives energy, aggressiveness, protection, success in combat, attack and sexual matters.

Jupiter gives good-luck, expansion, health, success in business, law, religion, medicine.

Saturn gives stability, concreteness, constriction, success with time, old people, antiques, land.

For a detailed list of rulerships, in order to know which Magic Square to use in which magical operation, a valuable manual is "The Rulership Book. A Directory of Astrological Correspondences" by Rex E. Bills, published in 1971 by the Macoy Publishing and Masonic Supply Co., Inc., of Richmond, Virginia.

Kamea of the Sun

A square of 36 boxes in 6 columns, 6 boxes in each column. Total of each line, 111. Total of all squares, 666.

6	32	3	34	35	1
7	11	27	28	8	30
19	14	16	15	23	24
18	20	22	21	17	13
25	29	10	9	26	12
36	5	33	4	2	31

Kamea of the Moon

A square of 81 boxes, 9 columns each with 9 boxes. Total of each line, 369. Total of all numbers, 3,321.

37	78	29	70	21	62	13	54	5
6	38	79	30	71	22	63	14	46
47	7	39	80	31	72	23	55	15
16	48	8	40	81	32	64	24	56
57	17	49	9	41	73	33	65	25
26	58	18	50	1	42	14	34	66
67	27	59	10	51	2	43	75	35
36	68	19	60	11	52	3	44	76
77	28	69	20	61	12	53	4	45

Kamea of Mercury

A square of 64 boxes, 8 columns of 8 boxes. Total of each line, 260. Total of all numbers, 2,080.

8	58	59	5	4	62	63	1
49	15	14	52	53	11	10	56
41	23	22	44	45	19	18	48
32	34	35	29	28	38	39	25
40	26	27	37	36	30	31	33
17	47	46	20	21	43	42	24
9	55	54	12	13	51	50	16
64	2	3	61	60	6	7	57

Kamea of Venus

A square of 49 boxes, 7 columns of 7 boxes. Total of each line, 175. Total of all numbers, 1,225.

22	47	16	41	10	35	4
5	23	48	17	42	11	29
30	6	24	49	18	36	12
13	31	7	25	43	19	37
38	14	32	1	26	44	30
21	39	8	33	2	27	45
46	15	40	9	34	3	28

Kamea of Mars

A square of 25 boxes, 5 boxes in each of 5 columns. Total of each line, 65. Total of all numbers, 325.

11	24	7	20	3
4	12	25	8	16
17	5	13	21	9
10	18	1	14	22
23	6	19	2	15

Kamea of Jupiter

A square of 16 boxes, 4 columns of 4 lines each. Total of each line, 34. Total of all numbers, 136.

4	14	15	1
9	7	6	12
5	11	10	8
16	2	3	13

Kamea of Saturn

A square of 9 boxes, 3 columns of 3 boxes each. Total of each line, 15. Total of all numbers, 45.

4	9	2
3	5	7
8	1	6

PLANETARY TABLES

Days and Hours

Sunday—Sun. Monday—Moon. Tuesday—Mars. Wednesday—Mercury. Thursday—Jupiter. Friday—Venus. Saturday—Saturn. On the days which they rule the Luminaries and Planets are particularly strong shortly after midnight, at dawn and for two hours thereafter, midafternoon and late evening around 10:00 P.M.

Powers

PLANET	RULES	DETRIMENT	EXALTATION	FALL
Sun	Leo	Aquarius	Aries	Libra
Moon	Cancer	Capricorn	Taurus	Scorpio
Mercury	Gemini	Sagittarius	Aquarius	Leo
Mercury	Virgo	Pisces		
Venus	Taurus	Scorpio	Pisces	Virgo
Venus	Libra	Aries		
Jupiter	Sagittarius	Gemini	Cancer	Capricorn
Jupiter	Pisces	Virgo		

Saturn	Capricorn	Cancer	Libra	Aries
Saturn	Aquarius	Leo		
Uranus	Aquarius	Leo	Scorpio	Taurus
Neptune	Pisces	Virgo	Leo	Aquarius
Pluto	Scorpio	Taurus		

Metals, Gems, Colors, Flowers

SUN — Gold. Yellow diamond, carbuncle, cat's eye, chrysolite, all golden colored stones. Gold, yellow, orange, white. Forsythia, goldenrod, heliotrope, juniper, marigold, mistletoe, peony, poppy, sunflower and any yellow or orange flower.

MOON — Silver, aluminum, Crystal, moonstone, pearl. Silver, white, pale blue. Daisy, honeysuckle, lilies, all white and pastel shaded flowers, night-blooming flowers.

MERCURY — Quicksilver. Opal, agate. Violet, lavender, opalescent hues. Azalea, lilac, moly (wild garlic), violet, all artificial flowers.

VENUS — Copper, bronze. Cornelian, emerald, turquoise. Green, yellow-green, blue-green, pink. Apple blossom, bleeding heart, clover blossom, columbine, daffodil, gladiolus, mock orange, myrtle, orange blossom, pansy, peach blossom, roses, sweet-pea, any sweet-smelling flower.

MARS — Iron, steel. Ruby, garnet or any red stone. Red, orange. Anemone, geranium, hollyhock, thistle and any bright red flower.

JUPITER — Tin. Lapis lazuli, amethyst. Blue, purple. Carnation, chrysanthemum, dahlia, hyssop, iris, oak leaves and acorns, poplar leaves, all evergreens.

SATURN — Lead. Onyx, jet. Black, grey, indigo. Century-plant, nightshade, sweet shrub, straw-flowers, all dried flowers.

Incense

SUN — Blood, dried grass, frankincense (olibanum), semen, all bright clean, sunny odors.

MOON — Dittany of Crete, honeysuckle, lily of the valley, menstrual blood, myrrh, wormwood, all dry virginal odors.

MERCURY — Jasmine, lavender, mace, mastic, storax, all subtle odors.

VENUS — Oil of cloves, honey, myrtle, rose petals, sandalwood, semen, vanilla, all sweet-smelling voluptuous odors.

MARS — Ammonia, blood, dragon's blood, patchouli, pepper, semen, sulphur, tobacco, turpentine, all hot, pungent, penetrating odors.

JUPITER — Almond, arnica, cedar, cinnamon, cinquefoil, oil of civet, musk oil, olive oil, saffron, sage, all expansive, pervasive odors.

SATURN   Dittany of Crete, scammony. Burning bone, feathers, hair. All
           earthy, musty odors, and odors of decay.

Sachet Ingredients

(Pulverized dried blossoms, fruit, seed, leaves, bark, root.)

SUN   Aloes, angelica, blueweed, cinnamon, dandelion, eucalyptus,
           eye-bright, hornwort, rue, spearmint.

MOON   Betony, endive, forget-me-not, moonwort, trefoil (three-leaved
           plant such as clover), watercress, willow, wormwood.

MERCURY   Anise, aniseed, bittersweet berries, calamint, calomel, carrawy
           seed, dill, elecampane, fennel, hazel, horehound, jasmine,
           marjoram, may apple, parsley, savory, valerian.

VENUS   Apple, apricot, birch, burdock, catnip, cherry, chickpea, clover,
           coltsfoot, cowslip, fern, figs, foxglove, ivy, lovage, mallow,
           myrtle, pennyroyal, plantain, sycamore, tansy, thyme, verbena,
           vervain, yarrow.

MARS   Barberry, basil, briars, bryony, catcus, capers, coriander, flax-
           seed, ginger, hops, horseradish, leek, mustard, nettles, onion,
           pepper, thorny plants.

JUPITER   Almond, balm, balsam, bay leaves, berries, bloodwort, blue flag
           (iris), borage, chervil, chestnut, chicory, cinquefoil, dock, gin-
           seng, hyssop, liverwort, olives, orris root, sage.

SATURN   Aconite, barley, beech, blackthorn, boneset, cereals, comfrey,
           cypress, dried fruits, hay, hellebore, bitter herbs, mosses, mush-
           rooms, rye, solomon's seal, wintergreen, wolfbane, yew.

TALISMANS

A talisman is a magical figure drawn in paint, water-color, ink or crayon
on parchment, leather, wood, metal, cloth or paper and charged with the
force which it is intended to represent.

Ritual for Making Talismans

Waxing Moon. On a day and at a time sacred to the luminary or planet
and when it is in the Sign which it rules or the Sign of its exaltation.

On the Altar are the four Magical Tools in their proper places and the
equipment and materials to make the talisman. For a Magic Square talisman,
parchment is best and the lines of the square should have already been drawn
heavily and the numbers filled in lightly so as to have a guide when they are
to be put in ceremonially. Flowers and candles of a color appropriate to the
luminary or planet may also be on the Altar, as may be the metal and gem.
Of course, the Magic Square is most appropriate when it is cut or scratched

on the proper metal, in which case a suitable stylus must be at hand. The gem may be worn as in a ring or pendant. On side table in south are Censer with charcoal and a container of appropriate incense with lighter or matches. Ritual Book on stand by chair in west. Another chair in east.

Perform Opening Exercises of Temple Rite, censing the Altar after the Sign of the Enterer.

Seated in the west, meditate on the purpose or objective of making the talisman, vividly visualizing a successful outcome. Then stand and repeat the "Holy art Thou" prayer, adding:

> Evohe! Evohe! Evohe!
> Ye Great Ones beyond and behind my being!
> Ye Old Ones out of the Night of Time!
> Great thou art and greatly to be honored.
> I honor thee! Honor thou me with thy presence or that of a messenger of thine!
> I ask a blessing on the magical task I am about to perform.

Call three times the name and title of the planetary force and the name of the spirit of the planet.

> (Sun) Sol! Sun! Lord of the Fire of the World! Sorath (so-RAHTH) spirit of the Sun!
>
> (Moon) Luna! Moon! Lady of the Night! Chasmodai (kahs-MODE-ah-ee) spirit of the Moon!
>
> (Mercury) Hermes! Mercury! Divine Messenger! Magus of Power! Taphthartharath (toff-THAR-thuh-rahth) spirit of Mercury!
>
> (Venus) Aphrodite (aff-ro-DYE-tee)! Venus! Lady of Delight! Daughter of the Mighty Ones! Kedemel (kee-DEM-el) spirit of Venus!
>
> (Mars) Ares! Mars! Lord of the Hosts of the Mighty! Bartzabel (BART-zuh-bel) spirit of Mars!
>
> (Jupiter) Zeus! Jupiter! Pan! Lord of the Forces of Life! Hismael (HISS-mah-el) spirit of Jupiter!
>
> (Saturn) Kronos! Saturn! Great One of the Night of Time! Zazel (ZAH-zell) spirit of Saturn!
>
> This is your day and this is your hour! You are in the Sign of your Rulership (Exaltation). Now you are powerful indeed! Everything obeys your will! Permit me to be your instrument! Make me your priest (priestess)!

Go from west by north to east. Spread hands over equipment and materials and say:

> These are not my hands, but those of (name and title of the planetary force) that do this work.

Take Rod and make widdershins circle over equipment and materials and say:

> Hekas! Hekas! Este Bibeloi! Be far from here, O ye profane! Banished be all occult and psychic influence and vibrations from this equipment and materials. I declare it to be virgin.

Make Circled Cross, saying:

I bless you in the name and charge you with the force of (name and title of the planetary force).

Sit. If the talisman is for a specific objective, name it three times. If the talisman is for a particular person, name that person three times. Then copy the correct numbers in the correct boxes of the Magic Square, beginning with 1 and continuing 2, 3, 4, 5, etc. Do it very carefully and very deliberately, slowly and with great intensity of will, feeling the force of the luminary or planet and repeating the name and title many times, perhaps with each number. (If a mistake is made, immediately exorcise the talisman and perform the Closing Exercises of the Temple Rite, postponing the ritual until the next favorable day.) After the talisman is correctly made, stand, hold high the talisman with both hands and repeat again the objective and/or the name and title. Replace talisman on Altar, trace the symbol of the luminary or planet in the air over it followed by the Circled Cross and say:

I declare this talisman to be charged with the force of (name and title). Blessed be!

Return to west, sit. Perform Closing Exercises of Temple Rite, omitting the widdershins circumambulation.

SIGILS

A sigil is the signature or seal of a Planetary Force in the form of a symmetrical design, often used in making talismans. Sigils are formed in many ways, the oldest in magical practice is that of making use of the Magical Squares or Kameas of the planets.

The requisite to tracing Sigils of the planetary names as formed from the Kameas is AIQ BEKER, or the Quabalah of Nine Chambers. By this method, the letters of the Hebrew alphabet are grouped together according to the similarity of their numbers. Thus in one Chamber, Gimel, Lamed and Shin are placed for their numbers are similiar—3, 30 and 300. The same rule applies to the others. The name of the method obtains from the letters placed in the first two Chambers. In the first Chamber are Aleph, Yod and Qoph, whose numbers are 1, 10 and 100, while in the second Chamber are Beth, Kaph, Resh—2, 20 and 200— thus AIQ BKR.

The Hebrew letters, phonetic prununiciation, their numbers and English equivalents are:

Aleph (AH-leff)	1	A
Beth (bayth)	2	B
Gimel (hard gee-mul)	3	G
Daleth (DAH-leth)	4	D
He (hay)	5	H, E
Vau (vahv)	6	V, U, O
Zayin (ZAH-yin)	7	Z
Cheth (hayth)	8	Ch
Teth (tayth)	9	T
Yod (yode)	10	I, Y, J
Kaph (kahf)	20	K
Lamed (LAH-med)	30	L
Mem (mayme)	40	M
Nun (noon)	50	N
Samech (SAH-mehk)	60	S

Ayin (AH-yin)	70	O or Ng
Pe (pay)	80	P
Tzaddi (TZAHD-ee)	90	Tz
Qoph (quof)	100	Q
Resh (raysh)	200	R
Shin (sheen)	300	Sh
Tau (tahv)	400	Th

Now in order to find the Sigil of a Name by using the Kamea, it is necessary to reduce the letter numbers to units by means of the above quoted scheme. For example, in the case of Zazel, the Spirit of Saturn, the letters are Zayin 7, Aleph 1, Zayin 7, and Lamed 30. Lamed reduces to 3, thus the numercial order of the letters is 7-1-7-3. The next step is to trace a line on the Kamea following the succession of the numbers. Thus, in the name of Zazel, the line would begin in box 7 of the Kamea of Saturn, go to 1, return to 7 again and then to 3. A little circle should be made at the beginning of the line on the first letter of the Sigil to show where the name begins. When a number is repeated a little loop is made.

SUN. Sorath, Samech 60, Resh 200, Aleph 1, Tau 400. 6-2-1-4.

MOON, Chashmodai. Cheth 8, Aleph 1, Shin 300, Mem 40, Daleth 4, Aleph 1, Yod 10. 8-1-3-4-4-1-1.

MERCURY. Taphthartharath. Teth 9, Aleph 1, Pe 80, He 5, Tau 400, Aleph 1, Resh 200, Tau 400, Aleph 1, Resh 200, Aleph 1, Tau 400. 9-1-8-5-4-1-2-4-1-2-1-4.

VENUS. Kedemel. Kaph 20, Daleth 4, Mem 40, Lamed 30. 2-4-4-3.

MARS. Bartzabel. Beth 2, Resh 200, Tzaddi 90, Beth 2, Lamed 30. 2-2-9-2-3.

JUPITER. Hismael. He 5, Samech 60, Mem 40, Aleph 1, Lamed 30. 5-6-4-1-3.

SATURN. Zazel. Zain 7, Aleph 1, Zain 7, Lamed 30. 7-1-7-3.

CASTING THE RUNES

Obtain four slats of wood each about five inches in length, about one-half inch in width and from one-eighth to one-fourth inch in thickness, such as are used for ice cream sticks. On one side of each of them paint a large black dot in the center of the stick. On the other side of each paint two large black dots so spaced as to divide the stick into three equal segments. These are your rune sticks. Consecrate them with the Ritual for Making Talismans using the names and titles associated with Mercury. Carry them about on your person for three days so as to imbue them with your magnetism. Then use them for divination.

In divining with the rune sticks it is most helpful to have a consecrated Magic Square of Mercury on the table or Altar along with (optional) flowers and candles and especially with an incense of Mercury. Before the divination hold the Mercurial Magic Square in both hands and enter the silence after saying:

Herne, Lord of the Crossroads! Thoth, Tahuti, Master of Wisdom!
Raphael, Gabriel, Messengers of Heaven! Hermes, Mercury, Magus
of Power! Juggler with the Secret of the Universe! Lend me thine
aid!

Or:

Lord Hermes, Messenger of Light!
Thee I invoke with all my might!
Messenger whose messenger I would be—
Thee I invoke, come thou unto me!

Or:

From a word to word may I be led to a word!
From a sign to a sign may I be led to a sign!

If divining alone the divination should be preceded and followed by the
Private Temple Rite.

Rune Stick Divination

Take a sheet of paper and write a question. Turn the paper over and lay
it on the Altar or table, blank side up. Take the rune sticks in the right hand
and cast them so they tumble away from you in parallel formation on the
surface before you. Thus they create a figure of four lines with one or two
dots on each line. Copy this figure in the upper right corner of the sheet of
paper. For example:

```
        .   .

      .

      .

    .   .
```

Throw the sticks three more times in the same manner and copy the
figures consecutively to the left of the first figure. Again for example:

4th Throw	3rd Throw	2nd Throw	1st Throw
.	. .	.	. .
.	. .	. .	.
.	. .	. .	.
.	. .	.	. .

These four figures are called the Mothers. From them are created a
second set of four figures called the Daughters. The first figure of the Daughters is made directly under the first Mother, on the right-hand side of the
paper, and consists of the top line of Mother 1, 2, 3, 4, placed each under the
other. For instance:

Top line of 1st Mother	. .
Top line of 2nd Mother	.
Top line of 3rd Mother	. .
Top line of 4th Mother	.

83

The other three Daughter figures are made in exactly the same way by taking the second, third and fourth lines of the Mothers and making figures of them thusly:

Daughter 4 **Daughter 3** **Daughter 2** **Daughter 1**

Daughter 4	Daughter 3	Daughter 2	Daughter 1
• •	•	•	• •
•	•	• •	•
• •	• •	• •	• •
•	•	•	•

We now have eight figures of four Mothers and four Daughters. Beginning with the first Mother and ending with the last Daughter, make another set of figures called the Resultants. These are produced by adding the dots laterally of the first and second figures, the third to the fourth, the fifth to the sixth and the seventh to the eighth. If the sum of the addition is an odd number note down a single dot. If the sum is an even number note down two dots.

Thusly:

Resultant 4 **Resultant 3** **Resultant 2** **Resultant 1**

Resultant 4	Resultant 3	Resultant 2	Resultant 1
•	•	•	•
• •	•	•	•
• •	• •	•	• •
• •	• •	•	•

The same process is applied again to produce two more figures called Witnesses. Laterally add the dots of the top lines of Resultants 1 and 2 to get the top line of the first Witness. Laterally add the second line of Resultants 1 and 2 to get the second line of the first Witness. Add the third line of Resultants 1 and 2 for the third line of the first Witness. Add the bottom line of Resultants 1 and 2 for the fourth line of the first Witness. Add the lines of Resultants 3 and 4 to produce the second Witness. Thus:

Witness 2 **Witness 1**

Witness 2	Witness 1
• •	• •
•	• •
• •	•
• •	• •

Finally repeat the same operation with the two Witnesses to produce the last figure called the Judge. Thus:

Judge

Judge
•   •
•
•
•   •

All of this seems complicated at first, but after a few trial runs it becomes quite easy.

The four Mothers show the positive, the "pro" side of the question. The four Daughters show the opposing, the negative, the "con" or "anti" side of the question. The four Resultants show the conflict of the problem. The two Witnesses show either the two main factors bearing upon the problem or the two possible courses of action. Finally the Judge gives his decision which indicates the outcome, result or definite answer to the question. The Judge's decision may be appealed or clarified by constructing still another figure called the Reconciler. This is made by adding the lines of the Judge to those of the first Mother.

Rune Meanings

VIA. Way, path, journey, connection.

POPULUS. People, group, crowd, the public.

PUELLA. Girl, woman, female.

PUER. Boy, man, male.

AMISSIO. Loss, demotion, unemployment.

ACQUISITO. Gain, promotion, job, work.

85

RUBEUS. Red, the dark one, winter, nighttime.

ALBUS. White, the light one, summer, daytime.

FORTUNA MAJOR. Great fortune, success, gift received, **upright cup.**

FORTUNA MINOR. Moderate fortune, some success, gift given, downturned cup.

CONJUNCTIO. Conjunction, wedding, face-to-face meeting, **partnership.**

CARCER. Restriction, bondage, lack of freedom.

TRISTITIA. Sorrow, bereavement, illness, pain.

.   **LAETITIA**. Joy, health, hopes and wishes, home, family.

. .
. .
. .
———

.   **CAUDA DRACONIS**. Dragon's tail, beginning, go, yes, up-
.   turned dagger.
.
. .
———

. .   **CAPUT DRACONIS**. Dragon's head, ending, stop, no, down-
.   turned dagger.
.
.
———

THE TREE OF LIFE

Preliminary reading: "The Mystical Qabalah" by Dion Fortune. Intro-
duction to "Kabbalah Unvailed" by S. L. MacGregor Mathers.
The Tree of Life is a glyph, a composite symbol, intended to represent
the cosmos in its entirety and the psyche of man as related thereto.

Negative Existence

The Tree has its origin in and is suspended from Negative Existence
which is impossible to comprehend because it is nothing, no-thing, absolute
zero, symbolized in this wise:

O
Ain
No. Absolute Negativity
OO
Ain Soph
No Thing
OOO
Ain Soph Aur
The Radiant Darkness, The Limitless Light,

The Flash of Lightning

Fom Ain Soph Aur, the Radiant Darkness, the Limitless Light, issues a

Flash of Lightning. Draw the Lightning Flash by connecting the periods of the numbers below in consecutive order:

1.

3. .2

5. .4

6.

8. .7

9.

10.

The Sephiroth

Along the path of the Lightning Flash appear ten emanations of deity called the Sephiroth. Each one is a Sephira. Ten are the Sephiroth, ten and not nine, ten and not eleven, ten are the Sephiroth. They are:

1. Kether, the Crown 2. Chokmah (HOKE-muh), Wisdom. 3. Binah (BEE-nuh), Understanding. 4. Chesed (HAY-sed), Mercy. 5. Geburah (ge-BOOR-uh), Severity. 6. Tiphareth (TIFF-uh-reth), Beauty. 7. Netzach (NET-zack), Victory. 8. Hod (rhymes with load and mode), Glory. 9. Yesod (YAY-sode), the Foundation. And 10. Malkuth (MAHL-kooth), the Kingdom.

On a nine by twelve inch (or larger) white cardboard draw ten one-inch in diameter circles, within which write the numbers and names in this wise:

1.
Kether

3.
Binah

2.
Chokmah

5.
Geburah

4.
Chesed

6.
Tiphareth

8.
Hod

7.
Netzach

9.
Yesod

10.
Malkuth

The Twenty-Two Connecting Paths

Twenty-two "Paths" connect the Sephiroth. Draw the paths with two straight lines a half-inch apart for each path. Draw and number them in this order:

Path 14 connects Binah and Chokmah, 3 and 2.

Path 19 connects Geburah and Chesed, 5 and 4.

Path 27 connects Hod and Netzach, 8 and 7.

Paths 13, 15, 17 and 25 are drawn as if under or behind Paths 14, 19 and 27, so when you make them, stop the lines as you come to these paths and then continue the lines on the other side.

Path 13 connects Kether and Tiphareth, 1 and 6.

Path 15 connects Chokmah and Tiphareth, 2 and 6.

Path 17 connects Binah and Tiphareth, 3 and 6.

Path 25 connects Tiphareth and Yesod, 6 and 9.
Finally, complete the Tree:

Path 11 connects Kether and Chokmah, 1 and 2.

Path 12 connects Kether and Binah, 1 and 3.

Path 16 connects Chokmah and Chesed, 2 and 4.

Path 18 connects Binah and Geburah, 3 and 5.

Path 20 connects Chesed and Tipareth, 4 and 6.

Path 21 connects Chesed and Netzach, 4 and 7.

Path 22 connects Geburah and Tipareth, 5 and 6.

Path 23 connects Geburah and Hod, 5 and 8.

Path 24 connects Tiphareth and Netzach, 6 and 7.

Path 26 connects Tiphareth and Hod, 6 and 8.

Path 28 connects Netzach and Yesod, 7 and 9.

Path 29 connects Netzach and Malkuth, 7 and 10.

Path 30 connects Hod and Yesod, 8 and 9.

Path 31 connects Hod and Malkuth, 8 and 10.

Path 32 connects Yesod and Malkuth, 9 and 10.

The Three Supernals

Kether, Chokmah and Binah are called the Three Supernals, the Supernal Triad. Kether is the One before whom no thing exists. Chokmah is God the Male. Chokmah is God the Father-Son. Chokmah is the Yod of Tetragrammaton. Binah is God the Female. Binah is God the Mother. She is the Great Mother, the Great Sea, the Anima Mundi, the First He of Tetragrammaton.

The Abyss

Below the Three Supernals, stretching across the Tree of Life, is a vast chasm called the Abyss. The Lightning Flash streaks across the Abyss, and reflects in Seven below that which in Three above. It changes polarity in crossing the Abyss.

Daath

Chokmah is Yang. Binah is Yin. Their conjunction is, becomes, and produces a Sephira which is hidden; a Sephira which has no number; a Sephira which is not shown on the path of the Lightning Flash. Its name is Daath, Knowledge. "To know" is here in the Biblical sense, as when a man "knows" his wife. Daath is the hidden union of Chokmah and Binah, of Yang and Yin, of Wisdom and Understanding. Daath is also the first and hidden product of that union. Daath is hidden by the Abyss. It is the "fall" of the angels and the "fall" of man.

Adam Kadmon

In their totality and unity the ten Holy Sephiroth represent the archtypal man, Adam Kadmon, the protogonos, called the Grand Man. The Tree of Life is often depicted as a human body, thus establishing the identity of Adam Kadmon, the Heavenly Man, the First Man, as the Idea of the Universe. The Sephiroth are analogous to the ten sacred members and organs of the Protogonos. Kether is the crown of the Prototypic Head. Chokmah and Binah are the left and the right hemispheres respectively of the Great Brain. Chesed and Geburah are the left and right arms respectively, signifying the active creative members of the Grand Man. Tiphareth is the heart, or according to some, the entire viscera. Netzach and Hod are the left and right legs respectively, or the supports of the world. Yesod is the generative system, or the foundation of form. Malkuth represents the two feet, or base of being. Occasionally Yesod is considered as the male and Malkuth as the female generative power.

Macrocosm and Microcosm

The human body, like that of the universe, is considered to be a material expression of the ten Holy Sephiroth. The non-physical or the supra-physical aspects of man, his soul, his mind, his spirit, like those of the universe, are likewise considered to be expressions of the ten Holy Sephiroth. Therefore man is called the Microcosm, the little universe, built in the image and likeness of the Macrocosm, the greater universe, of which he is a part.

Arikh Anpin

Kether, the Crown, is the Most High, the Ancient of Ancients. This is Arikh Anpin, Macroprosopus, the Vast Countenance.

Zoar Anpin

Chesed, Geburah, Tiphareth, Netzach, Hod and Yesod together are spoken of as Zoar Anpin, the Lesser Countenance or Microprosopus. This is the Vau of Tetragrammaton. Sometimes Tiphareth alone is spoken of as the Vau and as Zoar Anpin, but when this is done the other five Sephiroth are considered to be his appendages.

The Three Pillars

The Sephiroth are divided into three columns or pillars: the right-hand pillar of Mercy, consisting of the second, fourth and seventh emanations; the left-hand Pillar of Severity, consisting of the third, fifth and eighth emanations and the middle Pillar of Mildness, or Equilibrium, consisting of the first sixth, ninth and tenth emanations.

As we look at the Tree in the diagram we see Binah, Geburah and Hod upon the left side and Chokmah, Chesed and Netzach upon the right side. This is the way we view the Tree when we are using it to represent the Macrocosm. But when we use it to represent the Microcosm, that is our own being, **we back into it** so that the Middle Pillar equates with the spine, the Pillar that contains Chokmah, Chesed and Netzach with the left side, and the Pillar that contains Binah, Geburah and Hod with the right side. The Pillar of Severity is negative and the Pillar of Mercy is positive.

The Three Triangles

Nine of the Sephiroth naturally group themselves into three triads or triangles in each of which is a duad of opposite polarities or sexes and a uniting intelligence. The masculine and feminine potencies are the two scales of a balance and the uniting Sephira is the beam which joins them. In the Sephiroth there is a triple Trinity, the upper, middle, and lower. Kether, Chokmah and Binah form the upper Trinity, the Supernal Triad, the Supernals. This triad is called the Intellectual Triangle. Chesed, Geburah and Tiphareth form the middle Trinity, the Moral Triad. This is called the Ethical Triangle. Netzach, Hod and Yesod form the lower Trinity, the Astral Triad. This is called the Magical Triangle.

The Seven Planes

Seven are the Planes of Existence. In Being these are numbered from the Innermost to the Outermost, from the Highest to the Lowest. In Becoming they are numbered from the Outermost to the Innermost, from the Lowest to the Highest. The Ten Holy Sephiroth, singly or in pairs, correspond to the Seven Planes of Existence which are given various names by various schools. The correspondences and some of the names are:

I. - VII. Kether. Adi, the Absolute, the First Cause, the Divine Plane, World of God.

II. - VI. Chokmah - Binah. Anusadaka, the Monadic Plane, World of Virgin Spirits.

III. - V.   Chesed - Geburah. Nirvana, the Atomic Plane, World of Divine Spirits.

IV. - IV.   Tiphareth. Realm of Christ-Consciousness, the Buddhic Plane, the Intuitional World, World of Life Spirit.

V. - III.   Hod. The Mental Plane, World of Thought.
  A. Region of Abstract Thought, Buddhi-Manas, Realm of Spiritual Mind.
  B. Region of Concrete Thought, Manas, Realm of Mortal Mind.

VI. - II.   Netzach - Hod. The Astral Plane, the Desire World, the First Three Heavens, The Emotional or Psychic World, World of Action.

VII. - I.   Yesod - Malkuth. The Etheric-Chemical Plane, the Earth Plane.
  A. Yesod. The Etheric.
  B. Malkuth. The Physical World, the Chemical World, World of Matter, the Earth.

Each great Plane of Existence is divided into seven sub-planes. And each Sephira contains a whole Sephirotic sub-Tree. Actually the higher subdivisions of Netzach belong on the same Plane level as Hod, and only the lower subdivisions of Yesod belong on the same Plane level as Malkuth.

The Veil of Paroketh

Stretching across the Tree of Life between the level of Tiphareth and that of Netzach-Hod is a great veil called Paroketh. It separates the planes of force above from the planes of form below.

The Four Worlds

Four are the Worlds.

Four are the Worlds of the Macrocosmos of God.

Four are the Worlds of the Microcosmos of Man.

These are:

ATZILUTH, the Archtypal World, the Boundless World of Divine Names, the World of Emanations, the Divine World.

BRIAH, the Creative World, the Archangelic World of Creations, Khorsia the Throne, the World of Thrones.

YETZIRAH, the Formative World, the Hierarchal World of Formations, the World of Formation and of Angels.

ASSIAH, the Material World, the Elemental World of Substances, the World of Action, the World of Matter.

There are two groupings of the Sephiroth into the Four Worlds.
The first grouping is:

Atziluth, the Archtypal World. Kether.

Briah, the Creative World. Chokmah and Binah.

Yetzirah, the Formative World. Chesed, Geburah, Tiphareth, Netzach, Hod and Yesod.

Assiah, the Material World. Malkuth.

In the second method of classification all of the ten Sephiroth are considered as appearing in each of the Four Worlds upon another level of manifestation; so that just as Ain Soph Aur, the Limitless Light of the Unmanifest, concentrates a point, which is Kether, and the Emanations work down through increasing grades of density to Malkuth, so the Malkuth of Atziluth is conceived of as giving rise to the Kether of Briah; and so consecutively down the worlds, the Malkuth of Briah giving rise to the Kether of Yetzirah, and the Malkuth of Yetzirah giving rise to the Kether of Assiah.

The Archangels of Briah

Kether: Metatron, the Angel of the Presence.

Chokmah: Ratziel, the Herald of Deity.

Binah: Tzaphkiel, the Contemplation of God.

Chesed: Tzadkiel, the Justice of God.

Geburah: Samael, the Severity of God.

Tiphareth: Michael, Like Unto God.

Netzach: Auriel, the Light of God.

Hod: Raphael, the Healing of God.

Yesod: Gabriel, the Potent of God.

Malkuth: Sandalphon, the Messias.

The Orders of Angels of Yetzirah

Kether: Chaioth ha Qadesh, Holy Living Creatures.
Chokmah: Auphanim, Wheels.

Binah: Aralim, Mighty Ones, Thrones.

Chesed: Chasmalim, Brilliant Ones, Dominions.

Geburah: Seraphim, Fiery Serpents, Powers.

Tiphareth: Malachim, Kings, Virtues.

Netzach: Elohim, Gods, Principalities.

Hod: Ashim, Souls of Fire. Beni Elohim, Sons of God.

Yesod: Cherubim, Strong, Seat of the Sons.

Malkuth: Souls of Just Men made perfect.

The Spheres of Assiah

Kether: Rashith ha Galagalum, the Sphere of the Primum Mobile, the First Motion, the fiery mist which is the beginning of the material universe.

Chokmah: Mazloth, the Sphere of the Zodiac of Constellations, the Firmament of the Fixed Stars. As Space, this also is the Sphere of Uranus.

Binah: The Great Sea, the Sphere of Neptune.

Daath: Shabbathai, the Sphere of Saturn.

Chesed: Tzedeg, the Sphere of Jupiter.

Geburah: Madim, the Sphere of Mars.

Tiphareth: Shemesh, the Sphere of Sol, the Sun.

Netzach: Nogah, the Sphere of Venus

Hod: Kokab, the Sphere of Mercury.

Yesod: Levannah, the Sphere of the Moon.

Malkuth: Cholom Yosodoth, the Sphere of the Four Elements.

"Under the Earth" is the Sphere of Pluto.

The Tetragrammaton in the Four Worlds

The Yod of Tetragrammaton is Yah, the Supernal Father of Chokmah. The first He is the Supernal Mother of Binah. The Vau is Zoar Anpin or Tiphareth. This is the Bridegroom. The final He is Malkuth. She is the Princess, the Virgin, who becomes Kallah, the Bride, and then the Inferior Mother, Malkah the Queen. Her name in Magic is often Hertha, Mother Earth. The He final of Tetragrammaton is both twin sister and bride of the male child Vau.

The Color Scales

Traditionally there are four color scales of the Sephiroth in the Four Worlds—the King, Queen, Prince and Princess Scales. However, since the latter two are so rarely used and of such dubious value, we give only the King and Queen scales.

Sephira	King Scale	Queen Scale
Kether	Brillance	White
Chokmah	Pure soft blue	Grey
Binah	Crimson	Black
Chesed	Purple	Blue
Geburah	Orange	Red
Tiphareth	Amber	Golden yellow
Netzach	Pink	Emerald
Hod	Violet	Orange
Yesod	Indigo	Violet
Malkuth	Yellow	Citrine, russet, olive and black

MAGICAL CORRESPONDENCES
OF
THE TREE OF LIFE

The correspondences between the psyche of man and the universe are not arbitrary but arise out of developmental identities. Certain aspects of consciousness were developed in response to certain phases of evolution and therefore embody the same principles; consequently they react to the same influences. A man's soul is like a lagoon connected with the sea by a submerged channel. Although to all outward seeming it is land-locked, nevertheless its water level rises and falls with the tides of the sea because of the hidden connection. So it is with human consciousness. There is a subconscious connection between each individual soul and the World-Soul deep hidden in the most primitive depths of unconsciousness, and in consequence we share in the rise and fall of the cosmic tides. It is for this reason that divination is possible.

Each symbol upon the Tree represents a cosmic force or factor. When the mind concentrates upon it, it comes into touch with that force. In other words, a surface channel, a channel in consciousness, has been made between the conscious mind of the individual and a particular factor in the World-Soul, and through this channel the waters of the ocean pour into the lagoon. The aspirant to Higher Consciousness who uses the Tree of Life as a meditation symbol establishes point by point the union between his soul and the world-soul. This results in a tremendous access of energy to the individual soul. It is this which endows it with magical powers.

Path 1. KETHER, the Crown. The Admirable or Hidden Intelligence. Root of Air. The Life Principle. Mind. The Monad. The Atman. An ancient bearded king seen in profile.

Path 2. CHOKMAH, Wisdom. The Illuminating Intelligence. Root of Fire. God the Male. The Creative Force. A bearded male figure.

Path 3. BINAH, Understanding. The Measuring Intelligence. Root of Water. God the Female. The Great Mother. The Bitter Sea. A Matron.

Path 4. CHESED, Mercy. The Sanctifying Intelligence. Anabolic aspect of force. The loving, kind, righteous, magnaminous, majestic, merciful All-Father. A mighty crowned and throned king.

Path 5. GEBURAH, Strength or Severity. The Radical Intelligence. Catabolic aspect of force. Lord of Battles. God of Vengeance. A mighty warrior in his chariot.

Path 6. TIPHARETH, Beauty. Intelligence of the Mediating Influence. A King. A Sacrificed God. A male child.

Path 7. NETZACH, Victoy. The Occult Intelligence. The Anima. A beautiful naked woman.

Path 8. HOD, Splendor. The Resplendent Intelligence. The Mind. A hermaphrodite.

Path 9. YESOD, the Foundation. The Pure Intelligence. The libido. A beautiful naked man, very strong.

Path 10. MALKUTH, The Kingdom. The Absolute or Perfect Intelligence. The Gate. A young woman, throned and crowned.

Path 11. AIR. The Scintillating Intelligence. Pe, Mouth. Tarot Atu 0, the Fool.

Path 12. WATER. Intelligence of Transparency. Mem, Water. Tarot Atu XII, the Hanged Man.

Path 13. FIRE. The Illuminating Intelligence. Beth, House. Tarot Atu XX. Judgment.

Path 14. SATURN. The Uniting Intelligence. Cheth, Fence. Tarot Atu XXI, the Universe.

Path 15. LIBRA. The Constituting Intelligence. Tzaddi, Fish Hook, Tarot Atu VIII, Justice.

Path 16. TAURUS. The Triumphal Intelligence. Aleph, Ox. Tarot Atu V, the Hierophant.

Path 17. CANCER. The Disposing Intelligence. Daleth, Door. Tarot Atu VII, the Chariot.

Path 18. GEMINI. The House of Influence. Lamed, Ox Goad. Tarot Atu VI, the Lovers.

Path 19. LEO. The Intelligence of Will. Resh, Head. Tarot Atu XI, Strength.

Path 20. JUPITER. Intelligence of Activities of Spiritual Beings. Kaph, Palm of Hand. Tarot Atu X, the Wheel of Fortune.

Path 21. VIRGO. Intelligence of Conciliation. Yod, Hand. Tarot Atu IX. the Hermit.

Path 22. MARS. The Faithful Intelligence. Zayin, Sword. Tarot Atu XVI, the Tower.

Path 23. SCORPIO. The Intelligence of Probation. Ain, Eye. Taroa Atu XIII, Death.

Path 24. VENUS. The Imaginative Intelligence. Teth, Serpent. Tarot Atu III, the Empress.

Path 25. SUN. The Administrative Intelligence. Vau, Nail. Tarot Atu XIX. the Sun.

Path 26. MERCURY. The Stable Intelligence. He, Window. Tarot Atu I, the Magician.

Path 27. SAGITTARIUS. The Renovating Intelligence. Shin, Tooth. Tarot Atu XIV, Temperance.

Path 28. ARIES. The Natural Intelligence. Samech, Prop. Tarot Atu IV, the Emperor.

Path 29. PISCES. The Corporeal Intelligence. Nun, Fish. Tarot Atu XVIII, the Waning Moon.

Path 30. CAPRICORN. The Exciting Intelligence. Qoph. Back of Head. Tarot Atu XV, the Devil.

Path 31. AQUARIUS. The Collective Intelligence. Gimel, Camel. Tarot Atu XVII, the Star.

Path 32. MOON. The Perpetual Intelligence. Tau, Cross. Tarot Atu II, the High Priestess.

TREE OF MANY COLORS

The Tree of Life glyph you have made on the nine-by-twelve inch (or larger) cardboard is now ready to be painted, using oils, water colors, enamel paint, poster paint, or even crayons. Color the Sephiroth according to the Queen Scale and the connecting paths according to the following:

Unto Air is ascribed the Yellow of Tiphareth, unto Water is ascribed the Blue of Chesed, unto Fire the Red of Geburah, the colors of earth are to be found in Malkuth. The paths of the Planets are in the Rainbow Scale: Saturn is Indigo, Jupiter is Violet, Mars is Red, Sol is Orange, Mercury is Yellow, Venus is Green, and Luna is Blue. Unto the Zodiacal Paths are ascribed the following: Aries-Scarlet, Taurus-Red-Orange, Gemini-Orange, Cancer-Amber, Leo-Greenish-Yellow, Virgo-Yellowish-Green, Libra-Emerald, Scorpio-Greenish-Blue, Saggittarius-Blue, Capricorn-Indigo, Aquarius-Purple, and Pisces-Crimson.

The outlines of the circles of the Sephiroth, their numbers and names, and the elemental, planetary and zodiacal symbols on the connecting paths should be black. The symbol of Fire is an upward-pointing triangle, the symbol of Water is a downward-pointing triangle, that of Air is the upward-pointing triangle with a horizontal bar across it, Earth is the downward-pointing triangle with bar across it.

Frame the glyph and hang it on the eastern wall of your Temple. If you like, three other standard glyphs of the Tree of Life may be made as follows:

1. Draw and paint a Tree exactly like the above and superimpose a black serpent with tail below Malkuth, with body crossing every path from 32 to 11 but touching none of the Sephiroth, and head hovering near Kether.

2. Draw ten circles of the Sephiroth in proper order and instead of the Lightning Flash but with its same zig-zag course, draw a sword with its hilt extending beyond Kether and its point extending below Malkuth, painting the Sephiroth according to the King Scale.

3. Draw or trace the outline of a standing nude male figure and on it draw and paint the Sephiroth according to the description of Adam Kadmon, using the King Scale.

THE TREE OF LIFE IN THE AURA

In the aura which interpenetrates and surrounds the physical body, build up a replica of the Tree of Life.

It is best to build up the middle Pillar first. To do this, after the Opening Exercises of the Temple Rite, stand and raise yourself in imagination to your Kether by vividly visualizing a brilliant white light above your head while vibrating the Divine Name: Eheieh.

Imagine this light descending to Daath, at the nape of your neck.

Imagine the light pouring down into and flooding Tiphareth in your heart where it glows like sunlight and fills you with divine love and compassion. Sense this light radiating in all directions from your heart. Vibrate the Deity Name: Aloah va Daath.

In imagination, let the light descend gently unto Yesod in the region of the private parts and vibrate: Shaddai el Chai.

From Yesod visualize the light settling to Malkuth in which your feet are planted. Vibrate the Name: Adonai ha Aretz.

See and feel the light as a great pillar extending from above your head into the earth below your feet. Name it: The Pillar of Mildness in the midst of me!

Now visualize a great black pillar to your right. Don't turn your head, rather sense the pillar or glimpse it out of the corner of your eye. Flex the muscles of the right arm while vibrating: Elohim Gebor.

Sense strongly the presence of the black pillar while naming it: The Pillar of Severity to the right of me!

Next visualize a great white pillar to your left. Don't turn your head, rather sense the pillar or glimpse it out of the corner of your eye. Extend the left hand in a generous gesture of giving and vibrate the Name: El.

Sense strongly the presence of the white pillar while naming it: The Pillar of Mercy to the left of me!

Stand in glory for a moment, sensing strongly the three pillars. Then sit and enter the Silence.

Perform Closing Exercises of Temple Rite.

THE ALTAR OF THE MYSTERIES

Whereas the black-covered card table which we have been suggesting for use as an Altar has served its purpose well, a magically correct Altar will be henceforth needed. In a large lodge room or temple for group working the double cube Altar is "in proper proportion when it is the heighth of the navel of a six-foot man", but in a smaller room or private temple this size would be too large and cumbersome. Therefore make, or have one made, of a size and height convenient to you and in proportion to your private temple room. However the Altar should consist of two cubes, one on top of the other. It is traditional that each cube have one surface inwardly hinged so as to serve as a cupboard to store the Cup, Dagger, Disk, Censer, Incense, Candles, etc., when not in use. The wrapped Rod is always hidden elsewhere. The wood of the Altar should be oak. Both cubes should be painted black of a dull or flat finish on the outside, white on the inside. For the sake of maintaining ancient links a natural stone should be included somewhere in the Altar. The stone need not be at all large since it is purely symbolic and is to be kept in the bottom of the lower cube. This stone is sometimes taken from an ancient holy site. (Perhaps a pilgrimage to England, Greece, Israel or Egypt to secure a small flat stone from Stonehenge, Delphi, Elusis, Mt. Sinai or the Pyramids?) Or the Altar may have a marble top. When not in use the Altar top should be covered with a black cloth. The cover may be ornamental with gold tassles at the four corners, or it may have a gold fringe and a gold circled cross may be embroidered, appliqued or embossed on its center.

After the Altar is made and painted it is to be exorcised and dedicated when the Moon is approaching the Full and in an Earth Sign.

Altar in center of room empty and with nothing on it. On side tables against the walls are Rod, Censer with charcoal, lighter or matches and ashtray and container of Dittany of Crete in the south, Cup with water in the west, Dagger in east and Disk and the stone in the north. Chair in west. By it is stand with Ritual Book.

Enter, do not salute the Altar. Go directly to south, take Rod by female end and hold it upright in left hand, say:

El! Michael! Arahl!

Go widdershins from south to east to north to west. Say:

Elohim! Gabriel! Taliahad!

Go from west to south to east. Say:

Yahweh! Raphael! Chassan!

Go to north and say:

Adonai ha Aretz! Auriel! Phorlakh!

Go to west, change Rod to right hand and make counter-clockwise circle over top of Altar, saying:

By the Divine, Archangelic and Angelic Names of Fire, Water, Air, Earth, I exorcise this Altar of all contamination. Hekas! Hekas! Este Bibeloi! I declare this Altar to be virgin.

Go to south, replace Rod on side table, ignite the charcoal, proceed widdershins to west, sit. Read aloud:

The double cubical Altar in the center of the Temple is an emblem of the visible nature of the material universe concealing within herself the mysteries of all dimensions while revealing only her surface to the exterior senses. It is a double cube because, as the Emerald Tablet of Hermes has said, "The things that are below are a reflection of the things that are above." The world of created beings and things is a reflection of the worlds of divine beings and things. The Altar is referred to in the Sepher Yetzirah, the Book of Formation, as "an abyss of height and an abyss of depth, an abyss of the east and an abyss of the west, an abyss of the north and an abyss of the south." The Altar is black because, unlike divine beings who enfold in the element of light, the fires of created beings arise from darkness and obscurity. Such is the law, and so mote it be.

Stand and repeat the "Holy art Thou" prayer. Take Cup and sprinkle water over Altar, saying:

I purify this Altar with Water.

Replace Cup on stand in west, not on the Altar. Go deosil to south. Put incense in Censer and cense Altar, saying:

I consecrate this Altar with Fire.

Replace Censer. Take Rod in right hand and hold it high over Altar, saying:

El! Michael! Arahl!

Extend Rod to touch center of top surface of Altar and say:

This consecrated Rod represents the Yod of Tetragrammaton, the Element of Fire, and my will. I extend my will to this Altar that it may represent the basis of my work in Magic. Here may Light and Power find material manifestation. So mote it be!

Lay Rod on Altar. Proceed to west. Take Cup and hold it high over Altar, saying:

Elohim! Gabriel! Taliahad!

Lower Cup and say:

This consecrated Cup represents the first He of Tetragrammaton, the Element of Water, and my Love. I lay my love upon this Altar. May the Water of the Bitter Sea mingle with the springs of Mother Earth. That which has its inception in Binah has its culmination in Malkuth. So mote it be!

Place Cup on Altar. Go deosil to east. Take Dagger and hold it high over Altar, point upward, saying:

Yahweh! Raphael! Chassan!

Lower Dagger and say:

This consecrated Dagger represents the Vau of Tetragrammaton, the Element of Air, and my Life's-Breath. I dedicate my life anew to the holy quest of the Great Work! May Zoar Anpin claim his Bride. So mote it be!

Place Dagger on Altar. Go deosil to north. Take Disk and hold it high over Altar, saying:

Adonai ha Aretz! Auriel! Phorlakh!

Lower Disk and say:

This consecrated Disk represents the final He of Tetragrammaton, the Element of Earth, my Law and my body. In Magic, Love is the Law, Love under Will. May that law be embodied in me! Malkuth is in Kether and Kether is in Malkuth! And so mote it be!

Place Disk on Altar. Take stone and say:

With this stone there is a link with the ancient past. Firm and stable is this stone. Firm and stable is this Altar. One plus two plus three plus four equals ten. Ten is the number of Malkuth, the Kingdom. The tenth Path is the Absolute, or Perfect, Intelligence. This Altar represents to me the Perfect Path, the way of Theurgy. So mote it be!

Put the stone within the Altar. Go to east, spread hands over Altar and say:

By the Divine, Archangelic and Angelic Names of Fire, Water, Air, Earth, I dedicate this Altar as Beth-El, the House of God.

Make Circled Cross over Altar. Go to west, salute the Altar, sit.

Perform Closing Exercises of Temple Rite.

GATEWAY TO OTHER DIMENSIONS

In most Temples of the Mysteries and Lodges of the Adepts are to be found a pair of pillars usually called the Pillars of Hermes or the Pillars of Solomon. Like all symbols in Theurgy they are meant to lead the Seekers ever more inwardly toward Realization, Attainment, Satori, Mastery, Accomplishment of the Great Work. Primarily, they act as a gateway between levels or states of being and consciousness, they form a gateway to the Inner Planes.

You should now make, or have made, a pair of pillars for your private temple. They may range from beautiful pieces of furniture made by an expert woodworker to two painted broomsticks set upright on square bases. The pillars are traditionally square but may be rounded; the bases should be cubical and black; if at all possible the height should be at least a foot taller than the Theurgist; the pillars may have capitals on the tops; and one pillar is painted black, the other white. The dimensions should be in keeping with the size of the room, four to six inches in breadth and thickness is about right for an average size room.

The pillars should be exorcised and dedicated when the Moon is approaching the Full and in an Air Sign.

Pillars together with bases touching in center of room, black on the left, white on the right, when you are facing east. Altar against or close to eastern wall. Altar covered, nothing on it. Stand in south with Rod, Censer, charcoal, lighter and Galbanum incense or mixture of Lavender and Rose Petals. On stand by chair in west is the Ritual Book.

Enter, do not salute the Altar. Go directly to south, take Rod by female end and hold it upright in left hand, say:

El! Michael! Arahl!

Begin widdershins circumambulation around the pillars only. Do not include the Altar in the circumambulation. In the west, say:

Elohim! Gabriel! Taliahad!

Continue widdershins to east, say:

Yahweh! Raphael! Chassan!

Go to north and say:

Adonai ha Aretz! Auriel! Phorlakh!

Go to west, change Rod to right hand and touch each pillar, saying:

By the Divine, Archangelic and Angelic Names of Fire, Water, Air, Earth, I exorcise these pillars of all contamination. Hekas! Hekas! Este Bibeloi! Be far from here, O ye profane! I declare these pillars to be virgin.

Now take time out to rearrange the Temple. Imagine the western half of the room as containing the Sephira Malkuth in the center of which place the Altar. Place the pillars about two feet apart at the eastern edge of Malkuth at the beginning of Path 32. The black pillar is north or to your left as you face east, the white pillar is south or to your right. Thus the pillars are in the center of the room and the Altar is west thereof. On Altar are Rod in south, Cup with water in west, Dagger east, and Disk north, leave the Temple, re-enter, salute the Altar and—

101

Perform Opening Exercises of Temple Rite, igniting the charcoal in place of lighting the candle.

Stand and repeat the "Holy Art Thou" prayer. Take Cup and sprinkle water on both pillars, saying:

I purify these pillars with Water.

Go to south, put incense in Censer and cense the Altar in silence, then cense the pillars, saying:

I consecrate these pillars with Fire.

Replace Censer. Take Rod in right hand and holding it upright, circumambulate deosil the pillars three times so as to intone the Divine, Archangelic and Angelic Names of Fire in the south, Water in the west, Air in the east and Earth in the north. Finally stand before the pillars, facing east, and say:

By the Divine, Archangelic and Angelic Names of Fire, Water, Air, Earth, I dedicate and name these Pillars of Hermes and of Solomon to be the Gateway leading to Truth.

Touch black pillar with Rod and say:

This is the Pillar of Severity. This is Pingala. This is Yin. This is Boaz.

Touch white pillar with Rod and say:

This is the Pillar of Mercy. This is Ida. This is Yang. This is Joachin.

Point Rod eastward between the pillars and say:

This is the symbolical Gateway to the Immeasurable Regions. This is the Portal to other Dimensions of Consciousness and Being. It is watched over by the Guardian of the Threshold. None may go through save those who are worthy, well-qualified and duly and truly prepared. Such is the law. And so mote it be!

Return Rod to Altar. Go to west, sit. Read aloud:

The Gateway to Occult Wisdom and Magical Power is narrow, signifying that each one alone is responsible for his own advancement in the Mysteries. I seek Occult Wisdom. I aspire to greater Magical Power. I desire to explore the immeasurable Regions. I wish to experience other Dimensions of Consciousness and Being. But am I worthy? Am I well-qualified? Am I duly and truly prepared?

Sitting in the Silence, yearn to go through the Gateway. But go not near it.

Perform Closing Exercises of Temple Rite. Put things away. In moving the pillars for storage or other placement, go not between them.

WORTHY, QUALIFIED, PREPARED

The worthiness of the candidate for Initiation into the Mysteries is assumed. It is left to the Invisible Masters of the Inner Orders to do the judging. Suffice to know that if the candidate be unworthy, he will be turned back. Or even though he walk physically through the Gateway, nothing will happen.

Nevertheless it is well to consider the question of one's own worthiness before proceeding further. A great deal of sincere soul-searching is here called for. Perhaps a reading of "The Finding of the Third Eye" by Vera Stanley Alder would be helpful at this time.

In spite of the fact that you may be privileged to have already contacted either an earthly "guru" or "master" or one in another dimension, you should accept the fact that in the final analysis your own true personal master is your own personal Holy Guardian Angel. This is the term in Magic for what otherwise and elsewhere is known as the Self, the Oversoul, the I Am Self, the Christ Within, the Buddhic Self, the Divine Spark, the Atman, the Monad, the Spirit, that part of you which is divine and immortal, that part of you which is God. In Magic we seek "the Knowledge and Conversation of the Holy Guardian Angel." Strive then to be worthy in the eyes of your own Holy Guardian Angel.

But the Holy Guardian Angel is not the "Guardian of the Threshold." This, rather, is the "Anima" if you are male, the "Animus" if you are female, that part of your own psyche which is the "other", the opposite-polarity, side of you. Do not confuse this with the "shadow" which is the antithesis of your outward personality, your "persona." If these ideas are unfamiliar to you, by all means acquaint yourself with the writings of Carl Jung and Joseph Campbell. The Holy Guardian Angel is symbolized in Magic by Tarot Atu II, the Priestess, for males, and Tarot Atu I, the Magician, for females.

To be "well-qualified" is to possess at least the beginnings, the forerunners, indications, of magical maturity which includes a will of steel, intrepid fearlessness (which is **not** foolhardiness or adolescent "bravado"), a fervid but controlled imagination, a boundless love for all forms of life everywhere, a deep abiding faith in the essential goodness of the universe, and a willingness, nay, a determination, to accept responsibility for one's own being and actions. In short, to be well-qualified for magical advancement is to be a Pantheist. An eagerness to learn and a desire to be "more" than what presently one is, to grow, are indications of being well-qualified, as are intelligence and a sense of humor.

To be duly and truly prepared is to be well-read in occultism, pyschism, metaphysics, parapsychology and magic. **And** to have a certain amount of experience in magical practice. The rites, rituals and ceremonies so far given in this book, if performed and not just read, should have given sufficient experience. A rule of many magical fraternities is, "learn the theory before you attempt the practice." But the occult world is too full of theoretical occultists who are very well read indeed but who have no practical ability. Therefore the reader of this book is urged to learn the theory, yes, but also to attempt the practice.

Even if the candidate for the first degrees of Initiation be most worthy, he will still be turned back if he is not also well-qualified and duly and truly prepared. It is suggested that an extensive review of what has been read and learned so far and an attempt to clarify one's thinking and attitude toward Magic be now made.

THE RITE OF THE PORTAL

Waxing Moon changing from an Earth to an Air Sign. Fast for twenty-four hours before the Rite, taking only a little water.

Altar in center of room with the instruments in their proper places, Cup with water and a sprig of hyssop or mint. Also on Altar are Tarot Atu I, the Magician, and Tarot Atu II, the High Priestess. The pillars are halfway between Altar and eastern wall, black pillar north, white south, about two feet apart. Candle on stand against center of eastern wall. Censer with charcoal, lighter and mixture of Dittany of Crete and Galbanum (or Rose Petals and Lavender) on stand in south. Chair in west with stand and Ritual Book.

Perform Opening Exercises of Temple Rite, lighting the candle and igniting the charcoal. After entering the Silence, read aloud:

Long have I dwelt in Darkness. The Mother of Darkness hath blinded me with her Hair. The Father of Darkness hath hidden me under his Wings. My limbs are still weary from the wars which were in Heaven. The Voice of my Undying and Secret Soul said to me, "Let me enter the Path of Darkness, and peradventure there shall I find the Light. I am the only Being in an Abyss of Darkness; from an Abyss of Darkness came I forth ere my birth, from the Silence of a Primal Sleep." And the Voice of Ages answered to my Soul, "I am He who formulates in Darkness, the Light that shineth in Darkness, yet the Darkness comprehendeth it not."

Approach the Altar. Dip tips of thumb, forefinger and middle finger of right hand in water of Cup and touch them to forehead, saying:

Thou shalt sprinkle me with hyssop and I shall be cleansed. Thou shalt wash me and I shall be made whiter than snow.

Go deosil to south, put incense in Censer and cense Altar, saying:

May Adonai enkindle in me the fire of his love and the flame of everlasting charity.

Replace Censer. Go to west of Altar. Kneel on both knees and say:

Lord of the Universe! The Vast and the Mighty One! Ruler of the Light and of the Darkness! I adore thee and I invoke thee! Look with favor on this seeker who now kneeleth before thee, and grant thine aid unto the higher aspirations of my soul.

Remaining on knees, stare through the portals at the flame of the candle in the east. After a while, whisper:

He comes in the Power of Light!
He comes in the Light of Wisdom!
He comes in the Mercy of Light!
The Light hath healing in its wings!

Feel yourself flooded with Light. Either prostrate yourself flat on the floor with outstretched arms or remain on your knees for awhile adoring in silence.

You will begin to feel an attraction toward the pillars as if Something or Somebody on the other side of them is beckoning to you, silently calling to you, willing you toward the pillars. Get to your feet and take from the Altar the High Priestess and the Magician. Reverently kiss the Priestess and whisper to her:

O Guardian of the Threshold! Priestess of the Silver Star! Allow me to pass the Portal!

Reverently kiss the Magician and whisper:

O Magus of Power! Juggler with the Secret of the Universe! Give me the Keys to the Portal!

Replace the cards on the Altar. Staring through the pillars at the candle flame in the east, hear these words silently formulated:

Child of Earth! Long hast thou dwelt in Darkness. Quit the Night and seek the Day.

Wait until you are drawn, almost beyond your control, to the pillars, Standing before them, give the Sign of the Enterer. Step through the Gateway. Immediately on the other side of the Portal, assume the Crouch position: Squatting, elbows on knees, palms together, thumbs touching along nose, head bent (The seed is ready to sprout). Enter the Silence.

"Sink down, sink down, sink deeper and more deep
Into eternal and primordial sleep.
Sink down, be still, and draw apart
Into the inner earth's most secret heart.
Drink of the waters of Persephone,
The secret well beside the sacred tree . . .
Who drinks the waters of that hidden well
Shall see the things whereof he dare not tell—
Shall tread the shadowy path that leads to me—
Diana of the Ways and Hecate,
Selene of the Moon, Persephone."

A few minutes or several hours will pass. Afterward, give the Sign of Silence as you return back through the Portal and silently circumambulate widdershins, ending in the west. Put things away, get dressed, and

Have a feast. Blessed be!

RITUAL PATH WORKING

Required reading: "The Mystical Qabalah" by Dion Fortune. Consider this a must before beginning the Path workings. And before and after each Rite reread and meditate on the sections pertaining to the Sephiroth involved.

Rite of the Thirty-Second Path

Prerequisite: Ability to perform a Tarot or Rune Stick divination. Knowledge of influence of the Moon in the twelve Signs of the Zodiac and the twelve Houses of the Horoscope. Knowledge of the effects of the conjunction, parallel, sextile, trine, square and opposition aspects of the Moon to each of the Planets and the Sun. Experience in the performance of the Rite of the New Moon, the Full Moon Ceremony and the Ritual of the Portal.

Time: New Moon

On stand against eastern wall is a statue or picture of a muscular naked man with white candles on either side. On Altar in center of room are the four Magical Instruments in their proper places, Cup with white wine. Also on Altar are white or pastel flowers with a Tau Cross (a T-shaped cross) hidden among them, a consecrated Kamea of the Moon, and Atu II, the High Priestess. Pillars west of Altar and chair west of them. Ritual Book on stand next to chair. Incense: Dittany of Crete.

Robed, girded and sandled, enter Temple, salute Altar, light candles and ignite charcoal, go to west, sit. Pause. Then read:

> I am sitting in Malkuth of Assiah looking through the Portals of Solomon upon Path Thirty-two of the Tree of Life, the path that leads from Malkuth to Yesod. Malkuth, the Kingdom, is the Tenth Path of which the Sepher Yetzirah, the Book of Formation, says, "The Tenth Path is called Absolute, or Perfect, because it is the means of the primoridal which has no root by which it can cleave, nor rest, except in the hidden places of Yesod." This saying, as many others in Theurgy, I do not as yet understand. I hope to, and I shall, some day. On the Noble Eightfold Path this is Right Viewpoint. The hope and the will to attain—is this a right viewpoint for me? The Virtue here is Discrimination. Do I discriminate rightly? Do I choose wisely? (Pause in self-examination.) The Vice here is Indifference. To what am I indifferent? (Pause) How is this a vice? (Pause) Here in Malkuth I need help, oh, how I need help!

Stand and pray:

> Adonai Melehk, Lord who is King! Adonai ha Aretz, Lord of Earth! May I stand firmly upon the solid and sure rock of Right Doctrine and so have the Right Viewpoint of thy Kingdom! I ask for the blessing and assistance of the holy Angel Sandalphon in obtaining and maintaining true discrimination. May I avoid sluggishness and indifference. May I have the opportunities to develop, to have and to hold, the qualities of strength and endurance, stability, and practicality; to the end that I may perform the Great Work and so find myself to be one with thee! Amen.

Sit. Enter the Silence. Then read:

> The Thirty-second Path is before me. I desire to tread it, my desire is to experience it. But in order to do so I must be worthy, well-qualified, and duly and truly prepared. Am I worthy? (Pause.) Am I qualified and prepared? (Here review the Prerequisites above as if some authority or teacher were giving you an examination.) The Sepher Yetzirah says, "The Thirty-second Path is the Perpetual Intelligence because it rules the movements of the Moon according to their constitution, and perfects all the revolutions of the Zodiac and the form of their judgments."

Stand. Go to Pillars, give Sign of Enterer. Go through the gateway and proceed to Altar, genuflect, go deosil to south, cast incense upon the glowing charcoal and cense the Altar, replace Censer, go deosil to west, face Altar, take Tarot card, hold it high and say:

> O Priestess of the Silver Star! Iniatrix into the Mysteries! In your lap is the mystic scroll of the Akashic Records, the Memory of Nature! On your breast is the equal-armed cross. I aspire to the ability

to unroll and read that scroll! I aspire to achieve the balance of the four elements of my being so as also to wear the equal-armed cross! Lend me thine aid!

Replace card. Touch each of the four Instruments, saying:

Let Rod have rulership of right
To guide me on the Path of Light.
Let Cup be charged with competence
To fill me with benevolence.
Let Dagger be sharp and ever keen
To save me from all things unclean.
Let Disk be adequate and sure
To keep me faithful and secure.

Touch the card and say:

The Priestess of the Silver Star thus instructs the Candidate. "Know that the Holy Guardian Angel is attained by self-sacrifice and discipline. Purity is to live only to the Highest; and the Highest is All; be thou as Artemis to Pan."

Pause in contemplation of the High Priestess' words. Then touch the Kamea of the Moon and say:

O Lady of the Night! Artemis! Diana! Luna! Levannah! Maiden of Many Names! Great thou art and greatly to be praised! May your words sink deeply into my soul. May I share your Virtue of Contentment. May I, like you, go my way serenely. The Magic Powers you endow are Clairvoyance and Divination by Dreams. I would be greatly honored to receive these gifts from you!

Kneel and adore in silence. Then stand and say:

The Sin of this Path is Indolence. Indolence! A polite word for laziness. I vow henceforth to avoid this sin. The Vice of this Path is Idleness. I vow henceforth to avoid this vice. So here and now let willing hands be dedicated. (Spit on right hand.) Blessed be the hand put forth with might. (Spit on left hand.) Blessed be the hand put forth in meaning. (Rub hands together vigorously.) Blessed be what I must do with might and meaning that my hands may hold the harvest of my highest hopes.

Take Cup, hold it high and say:

The pale wine of the New Moon.

Spill a little wine onto the flowers, saying:

I offer fermented juice of the pale grape to the Lady of the Night.

Discover the Tau Cross. Say:

What's this! A gift from the Lady! A Tau! What can it mean? Thank you my Lady! I drink to you!

Drink the wine. Replace Cup. Examine Tau Cross and say:

This token from the Lady is a Tau. Tau is a Hebrew letter. It means cross. Cross! She has an equal-armed cross on her bosom. Cross! What can it mean? Perhaps she is telling me something. Perhaps she is showing me the way.—The way—of the cross—leads—home! The way of the cross leads home!

Dance deosil around Altar, singing or chanting three times:

The way of the cross leads home!
The way of the cross leads home!
It is sweet to know
As I onward go—
The way of the cross leads home.

Finish dance in the west. Sit, enter the Silence. Perform Closing Exercises of Temple Rite. Wear the Tau Cross on your person until Full Moon. Sleep with the Kamea of the Moon under your pillow every night and remember to record your dreams every morning until Full Moon. Practice various forms of Visualization and various techniques of inducing Clairvoyance every day until Full Moon. On the night of the Full Moon perform the Full Moon Ceremony and follow with the Dreaming True method as given in Portfolio of Magic.

Rite of the Thirty-First Path

Prerequisite: Ability to erect and delineate an Astrological natal chart. Performance of the Rite of the Thirty-second Path.

Time: Moon waxing in Aquarius.

On stand against eastern wall is a statue or picture of Hermes or Mercury or Tarot Atu I, the Magician, with white or lavender candles on either side. On floor or footstool before this is a potted plant with an artificial butterfly or bird perched on its top. On Altar are Tarot Atu XVII, the Star, in center, Cup with water in west and Dagger in east. Roses or Aspen leaves or Spanish Moss or Sprigs of Peppermint are scattered over Altar or may be in low vases, north and south. Hidden under the cup is a small piece of parchment or paper on which has been drawn the symbol of Aquarius and the Hebrew letter Gimel with this message written, "Use all thine energy to rule thy thought." Pillars west of Altar and chair west of them. Ritual Book, Horoscope Blank, Ephemeris of the current year, Tables of Houses, work sheet, watch or clock and pen or pencil on stand by chair. A small electric fan or air circulator to create a gentle breeze would be most appropriate. Incense: Galbanum if possible, otherwise Rose Leaves and Lavender.

Sky-clad, perform Opening Exercises of Temple Rite, censing Altar after Sign of the Enterer.

Seated in the west, after entering the Silence, read aloud:

I am sitting in Malkuth of Assiah, looking through the Portals upon Path Thirty-one that leads from Malkuth to Hod. The Sepher Yetzirah says, "The Thirty-first Path is the Collecting Intelligence, and it is so called because Astrologers deduce from it the judgment of the Stars and of the Celestial Signs and the perfection of their science according to the rules of their resolutions." I am an Astrologer. To demonstrate this I shall set up a chart for this very moment. (Do so quickly but accurately.) Moon is in Aquarius now and the Path before me and this Rite are dedicated and attributed to Aquarius. Wheras Astronomers and some Astrologers declare the Age of Aquarius to be a long time in the future, as far as I am concerned I'm in the Age of Aquarius right now. (Stand.) The Age of Aquarius! The Age of Freedom! Free from the shackles of time and space! Free from the limitations of the physical! Free from the oppressions of false theologies, power-structure ideologies, hypocritical moralities! Freedom to be! Freedom to become! Freedom to do! Freedom to live and let live, to love and let love! Do what thou wilt shall be the whole of the law, for love is the law, love under will!

Dance deosil lightly and joyously around Altar singing "The Age of Aquarius" from "Hair" or any other light and airy song such as "Funiculi Funicula." Finish dance in the west, face Altar, take the Tarot card, hold it high and say:

Daughter of the Firmament! Dweller betwen the Waters! Holy thou art, pure and innocent! You see clearly for your eyes are not dimmed by self-interest. I pray for the Gift of Spiritual Insight. (Replace card on Altar. Kneel.) Uranus! Lord of Magic! When Time began to rule you withdrew into the far recesses of Timelessness and Spacelessness. From that vantage point you see clearly, oh so clearly. Endow me with clearness of vision, give me realization of the possibilities, the human potential, both in myself and in others! (Pause in yearning. Stand. Touch card.) This is the Imagination of Nature. This is Aquarius the Waterbearer. I see the Waterbearer as a giant male figure, feet wide apart, in his arms a great urn or vessel from which he is pouring cool, clear water upon parched, dry earth. (Vividly visualize.) I see the Waterbearer as Ganymede, the Cupbearer, the beautiful boy beloved of Zeus. (Vividly visualize.) I see the Waterbearer as Aeolus, God of the Winds. (Vividly visualize.) I see the Waterbearer as Juno, Lady of Air. (Vividly visualize.) I see the Waterbearer as the Star of the Tarot. (Gaze at the card for a moment, then kneel, imitating her pose. Hold this pose for a moment, then stand, take the Cup and hold it high. Circumambulate deosil the Altar, carrying the Cup, watering the plant in the east.) I, too, am a Waterbearer! (In replacing the Cup discover the small sheet of parchment or paper.) What's this? A note! Perhaps a message? What is it? The symbol of Aquarius. A Hebrew letter. Gimel. And these words—"Use all thine energy to rule thy thought." Hmmmm! Use all thine energy to rule thy thought. The Hebrew letter is Gimel which means Camel. This must be a signature or a clue or a key. The number Gimel is three. The third Sephiroth is Binah, the Water above the Firmament. A Camel is a pack animal, a means of transportation, associated with deserts, dry places where there is little or no water. And the Camel is supposed to be able to go long distances without water. I presume he takes long drinks and carries his water with him. A Waterbearer! Here I am on the Thirty-first Path. Behind me is Malkuth. Before me is Hod which is on the Pillar of Severity headed by Binah! In order to bring the Waters of Truth from Binah above to Malkuth below I must use all my energy to rule my thought! (Pause.) Thank you, Great Ones beyond and behind my being! (Pause.) The Vice of this Path is Argumentation. This I promise to avoid. The Virtue of this Path is Altruism. This I promise to cultivate.

Dance again around the Altar, singing the same song. Finish dance in the west. Sit, enter the Silence, perform Closing Exercises of Temple Rite.

Rite of the Twenty-Ninth Path

Required reading: "Mysticism" by Evelyn Underhill. Prerequisite: The Rite of the Thirty-first Path.

Time: Near midnight with **waning** Moon in Pisces.

On stand against eastern wall is a statue or picture of Venus or Tarot Atu III, the Empress, with green candles on either side. On center of Altar is a goldfish bowl or aquarium with two live fish and green water plants, Cup with water in west, a bitter herb such as watercress, container of salt and Disk in north. Scattered on top of Altar are sea shells and seaweed or water plants with a natural or cultured pearl among them and a dried or artificial scarab or beetle or crayfish in the east. Pillars east of Altar. Ritual Book on stand by chair in west. Incense: Myrrh.

Robed, hooded, girded and sandaled, enter Temple, salute Altar, go by north to east, light candles, go to south, ignite charcoal, go to west, sit with hands clasped, thumb tips touching opposite palm, head bowed. Long pause. Then take Ritual Book and read aloud:

> I am sitting in Malkuth of Assiah, looking upon Path Twenty-nine that leads from Malkuth to Netzach. Immediately before me is water with fishes and water plants. Beyond are two towers. The Sepher Yetzirah says, "The Twenty-ninth Path is the Corporeal Intelligence and is so called because it forms the very body which is so formed beneath the whole order of the worlds and the increment of them." To Path Twenty-nine is ascribed the Zodiacal Sign of Pisces the Fishes, the Hebrew letter Nun which means Fish, and Tarot Atu XVIII, the Waning Moon.

> Here is a quest that calls me,
> This night when I am lone,
> The need to go where the ways divide
> The Known from the Unknown.

Stand. Circumambulate deosil slowly to south, saying:

> This is the Path of the Imponderable Forces of Nature. Here I find the place, the tenuous rim where the Seen g r o w s dim and the Sightless hides its face.

Cast incense upon the glowing charcoal and cense the Altar, saying:

> (Censing left.) Evohe! Evohe! Poseidon!
> (Censing right.) Evohe! Evohe! Neptune!
> (Censing front.) Evohe! Evohe! Lord of the Deep!

Replace Censer. Go to west, face Altar, take Tarot Card, hold it high and say:

> Ruler of Flux and Reflux! Child of the Sons of the Mighty! Older than night or day yet younger than the babe new born! Ever changing yet ever the same! Male and female, both and neither! Father who is the mother, mother who is the father! Parent who is the child, child who is the parent! Reveal to me your Mystery!

Lower card and gaze intently at it for a moment. Then say:

> It is Night. The Waning Moon is overhead. Tears are dropping. Below is Water. Life in the form of a crayfish (beetle) is emerging out of the water onto a much-trodden path. Bitter plants grow beside the water. The path traverses cultivated fields until it passes

between two grey towers of nameless mystery, beyond which is a dark foreboding forest and high dark menacing mountains. A wolf and a jackal are sitting at the base of the towers, baying the Moon. I can hear them! (Pause, listen!) The howling of wild animals —a beast of prey and a scavenger of rotting carcasses! Something— or somebody—is hiding behind a tower, lurking there, furtively watching me, perhaps waiting for me. Dark shadows beyond the towers are m o v i n g stealthily—now still as death, now darting quickly, now still again, now moving so very slowly. It's getting darker, the Moon gives no light. (Close eyes and vividly visualize the scene. Pause. A "horror of great darkness" will come upon you.) Anubis! Watcher at midnight! Jackal-headed god of Khem who stands upon the threshold! This is the threshold of life, this is the threshold of death! Lend me thine aid! Go before me and lead the way!

Replace card on Altar. Circumambulate deosil while saying:

There is a budding morrow in midnight. Let the Illusion of the World pass over me, unheeded, as I go from the Midnight to the Morning.

Returned to the west, face Altar and say:

The Vice of this Path is Worry. May my evergrowing, ever-deepening, ever-abiding Faith in the Great Ones beyond and behind my being prevent me from indulging in this vice. The Virtue of this Path is Sympathy. May I have sympathy like that of the Angels of Heaven! (Put a pinch of salt in the water of the Cup.) Salt are the tears and bitter is the taste of the Dark Night of the Soul. (Eat the bitter herb. Drink the salted water.) Yet how splendid is the adventure (Find and pick up the pearl) for in the midst of suffering and pain can be found the Pearl of Great Price! (Salute the figure on the stand in the east.) Hail the Morning Star!

Sit. Enter the Silence. Perform Closing Exercises of Temple Rite.

Rite of the Thirtieth Path

Prerequisite: Rite of the Twenty-ninth Path.

Time: Waxing Moon in Capricorn. If possible, on a Saturday.

Black Pillar in northeast corner of room, white Pillar in southeast corner. Before black Pillar, facing southwest, is stand with statue or picture of Hermes or Mercury or Tarot Atu I, the Magician, with lavender candles. Altar in center of room, so placed that its eastern side faces the northeast corner of room. For the centerpiece on the Altar use your ingenuity in devising a "Secret Flame". This may be a miniature red-globed oil lamp or a small candle in a ruby-red glass bowl. Put two oval or round stones beside it, or two hickory nuts. On Altar are the four Magical Instruments in their usual places, Cup with red wine. Also on Altar are Tarot Atu XV, the Devil, a consecrated Kamea of Saturn, a ballpoint pen of black ink, and pine cones with ivy or evergreen branches. Chair in southwest, facing northeast. Ritual Book on stand by chair. Kernunnos Incense (See Portfolio of Magic.) or Dittany of Crete or Scammony.

After bathing prior to rite, anoint throat, wrists, genitals and feet with natural or synthetic Oil of Musk.

Sky-clad or robed, girded and sandaled, enter Temple, salute Altar, light candles and lamp of the Secret Flame, ignite charcoal, go to chair, sit. Pause. Then read aloud:

> I am sitting in Yesod, in the Sphere of Levannah the Moon, looking upon Path Thirty that leads from Yesod to Hod. According to the Sepher Yetzirah the Thirtieth Path is the Exciting Intelligence because thence is created the spirit of every creature under the supreme Orb, and the assemblage of them all. To Path Thirty is assigned the Zodiacal Sign of Capricorn, the Goat, the Hebrew letter Qoph which means Back of the Head, and Tarot Atu XV, the Devil.

Stand, go to south of Altar, cast incense upon the coals, and cense Altar, saying:

> (Censing left.) Eko, Eko Azarak!
> (Censing right.) Eko, Eko Zomelak!
> (Censing forward.) Eko, Eko, Kernunnos!

Replace Censer. Go to southwest, face Altar, take Tarot card, hold it high and say:

> Lord of the Gates of Matter! Child of the Forces of Time! Khem! Set! Priapus! Pan!
>
> Hear me, Lord of the Stars!
> For thee I have worshipped ever
> With stains and sorrows and scars,
> With joyful, joyful Endeavor.
> Hear me, O lilywhite goat
> Crisp as a thicket of thorns,
> With a collar of gold for thy throat,
> A scarlet bow for thy horns.
>
> Thou art the Generative Power! Thou art Creative Force! (Lower card, stare at it for a moment.) The Sign of Capricorn is rough, harsh, dark, even blind; the impulse to create takes no account of reason, custom, or foresight. It is divinely unscrupulous, sublimely careless of result. (Pause.) O Man-Goat of Mendes, I hear your words—"Thou hast no right but to do thy will. Do that, and no other shall say nay. For pure will, unassuaged of purpose, delivered from the lust of result, is every way perfect."—I hear and I obey.

Replace card. Touch Kamea of Saturn and say:

> Old One of the Night of Time! Kronos! Saturn! Your Sphere is Shabbathai for you are the Old Lord of the Sabbath! May I truly observe and celebrate the Sabbath. Mark me with your sign! (Take pen in right hand and make symbol of Saturn on left palm, replace pen, fold middle and ring fingers of left hand to hide the symbol, holding them with thumb, extend forefinger and little finger.) It is not I that make this sign, it is Zazel, the Spirit of Saturn, that makes it. The Sign of the Old One! In it is power!

Look at and genuflect to the Secret Flame on the center of the Altar, saying:

112

The Secret Flame burns in the Stones of Adam Kadmon, powering the Machinery of the Universe. (Take one or both of the stones or nuts, warm it or them at the flame and apply to back of skull at nape of neck and to private parts.) May my Instincts be sharpened! May my Creative Force be strengthened! Vesta, Vesta, be strong in me; and as I will, so mote it be! (Replace stones on Altar.)

Dance deosil around Altar singing a song of aspiration such as "The Impossible Dream" or "Climb Every Mountain". Let leaping or jumping be included in the dance, imitating the fondness of the goat for high places. Finish dance in southwest, face Altar and say:

I have climbed the high place! The high places I shall ever seek for they are home to me as my true race is of the starry skies. Yet I despise not the low places, nor the places in between. All places and all things are habitations and expressions of the One who is the All! Therefore I shall search to find, to have and to hold, complete appreciation of all existing things. The Vice of this Path is Deceitfulness. Henceforth I abhor and foreswear all deceit! The Virtue of this Path is Diplomacy. I shall try to be diplomatic in all my relationships with all forms of life everywhere. To this end I drink. (Drink the wine in the Cup.) Such is my will, and so mote it be!

Sit. Enter the Silence. Perform Closing Exercises of Temple Rite.

Rite of the Twenty-Eighth Path

Prerequisite: Rite of the Thirtieth Path.

Time: Waxing Moon in Aries. If possible, on a Tuesday.

Black Pillar in northeast corner of foom, white Pillar in southeast corner. Before white Pillar is a stand, facing northwest, with statue or picture of Venus or Tarot Atu III, the Empress, flanked by green candles and with, if desired, a Victory Wreath of laurel leaves. Altar in center of room, so placed its eastern side faces the southeast. On Altar is tall red candle in holder. Tarot Atu IV, the Emperor, consecrated Kameas of Mars and the Sun, and the four Magical Instruments in their usual places, Cup with red wine. Scattered over Altar or formed in a wreath around base of candle or in low vases is a profusion of red flowers. Chair in northwest, facing southeast. By its side is stand with Ritual Book. Incense: Dragon's Blood if possible, otherwise Frankincense.

Perform Opening Exercises of Temple Rite, lighting the candles and igniting the charcoal after the Sign of the Enterer. Seated, read aloud:

Following the Path of the Serpent, I am in Yesod facing Path Twenty-eight which leads from Yesod to Netzach. According to the Sepher Yetzirah the Twenty-eighth Path is the Natural Intelligence because by it is perfected the nature of all things under the Orb of the Sun. To Path Twenty-eight is assigned the Zodiacal Sign of Aries, the Ram, the Hebrew letter Samech which means Prop, and Tarot Atu IV, the Emperor. The theme and aim of this Path is Action, but action that is wisely directed to the end of attaining Power, Authority, Leadership. Henceforth, I want no action that is without purpose. I will myself to never forget this.

113

Stand, circumambulate to south, put incense in Censer and cense Altar, saying:

(Censing left.) Ave (AH-vay) Mars, Ruler of Aries!
(Censing right.) Ave Sol, Great Sun, exalted therein!
(Censing forward.) Ave Michael, Archangel of Fire!

Replace Censer, go to southwest, face Altar, take Tarot card and hold it high, saying:

Son of the Morning! Chief Among the Mighty! Self-confident you are, frank, courageous and independent. (Lower card and gaze at it for a moment.) In Alchemy this card represents Sulphur, the male fiery energy of the Universe. In the Hindu teachings this is Rajas. It is the swift creative energy, the initiative of all Being. The power of the Emperor is a generalization of the paternal power. He bears a sceptre and an orb surmounted by a Maltese cross, signifying that his energy has reached a successful issue, that his government has been established. May it be so with (here name those potential "fathers"—whether of a child, a cause, an organization or a government—for whom you wish success.) and with me. (Again hold the card high, then replace it on Altar.)

Touch Kamea of Mars and say:

Mighty Mars, Ruler of Aries! Horus, Crowned and Conquering! Militant you are, energetic, enthusiastic and impulsive. Share your power with (Repeat name or names as above.) and with me, as you did in generous measure with Alexander the Great, Julius Caesar, Richard the Lion-Hearted, Napoleon Bonaparte and many another.

Touch Kamea of the Sun and say:

Exalted is Sol, the Sun, Father and King of the Solar System. Solar Logos! Word of the Father! Holy Avatar of God! God made manifest in human form! Osiris! Rama! Krishna! Jesus the Christ! Gautama the Buddha! Exalted you are, exalted you will ever be! (Kneel.) I worship thee and await thy again coming! (Adore in silence for a moment, then arise.) How may I serve and follow thee? How may I prepare for thy coming? (Pause.) Thus said the Lord to me, "Set fire to thyself; thus shalt thou become a Burning and a Shining Light." So be it, Lord. Thy word is law. (Cup hands around candle flame.) Burn, fire, burn! As you burn upon the Altar burn thou in me!

Dance, march or strut deosil around Altar, cadence-counting or shouting or singing a victory song, anything from your old school song to "The Battle Hymn of the Republic." Finish dance in northwest, face Altar, take Cup and hold it high, saying:

Achieve every possibility. Find thyself in every Star! The essence of this rite is the urge that impels to a new cycle with new ideas, new plans, new thoughts, new proposals—leading to victory. (Extend Cup toward Netzach.) To Victory! (Drink. Replace Cup.) The Virtue of this Path is Determination. May this virtue ever be mine! The Vices of this Path are officiousness, egotism, rashness. I avoid them like the plague. The Magic Powers of this Path are the Ability to Rule and the Power of Consecrating. To the one I aspire, I have already expressed the other. (Take Rod and hold it high.) I have said what I have said. By the power of Yah, the Yod of Tetragrammaton and the Wand of Will, so mote it be!

Replace Rod. Sit. Enter the Silence. Perform Closing Exercises of Temple Rite.

Rite of Paths Twenty-Five and Twenty-Seven

Required reading: "New Model of the Universe" by P. D. Ouspensky. Prerequisite: Rite of the Twenty-eighth Path.

Time: Waxing Moon in Sagittarius.

The "Veil of Paroketh" reaches completely across the eastern wall. This may be ceiling-to-floor drapes entirely covering the wall with an opening in the center, it may be tokened with ordinary gauze-type window curtains hung at the center of the wall, of it may simply be visualized as being beyond the eastern wall. Behind or beyond the Veil is a Crucifix, a cross with a corpus, in center of wall. In case the Veil is visualized the Crucifix may be on a stand against eastern wall and covered with a veil or a handkerchief, or the Crucifix may be fastened to the eastern wall and veiled. Against center of southern wall is a stand with statue or picture of Venus or Tarot Atu III, the Empress, with green candles. Beside it to the east is the white Pillar. Against center of northern wall is a stand with statue or picture of Mercury or Tarot Atu I, the Magician, with lavender candles. Beside it to the east is the black Pillar. On Altar in center of room are a bouquet of yellow (or orange) and purple flowers (iris if possible), four tall white candles in holders at the four corners and the four Magical Instruments in their proper places, Cup with water. Also on Altar are Tarot Atu XIV, Temperance, Tarot Atu XIX, the Sun, consecrated Kameas of Jupiter and the Sun, a nail, a bow and arrow which may be a child's toy since the use is symbolic, and two brandy glasses, snifters or tumblers, one of which contains a small amount of brandy. Chair in west, facing east. By it is stand with Ritual Book. Incense: a mixture of equal parts of Frankincense and Myrrh.

Robed, girded and sandaled, enter Temple, salute Altar, circumambulate deosil, lighting candles in north and on northwest and northeast of Altar, candles in south and on southeast and southwest of Altar, igniting charcoal, then returning to west. Sit Pause. Read aloud:

> I am in Yesod. Before me is a crossroad. From Hod in the north on my left to Netzach in the south on my right, is Path Twenty-seven. Directly before me, l e a d i n g from Yesod to Tiphareth, is Path Twenty-five. The Paths cross in the center of the Temple, where stands the Altar. A crossroad! The witches, or rather the wicca, the wise ones, used to sometimes meet at a crossroad, a place where roads cross. Esoteric tradition affirms that when the pupil is ready, the master appears. It further affirms that the Inductor into the Mysteries, the Hierophant, the Wise One, the Teacher, the Mother of Wisdom, is met at a crossroad, where roads cross. This Rite I am now performing signifies such a meeting and its performance sets the imponderable forces at work to bring such a meeting about. Now I can start looking for the Stranger Who Can Show the Way at crossroads, anywhere from the crossing of two dusty dirt roads or lanes far out in the country to the intersection of Forty-Second

Street and Broadway in New York or Hollywood and Vine in Los Angeles. But why does it have to be a stranger? Perhaps it is someone I already know. I rather think, however, that the crossroads refer to a climax or time of choice of direction in one's life. Am I at a crossroads of my life? (Pause.) Is this a time of change of direction for me? Is there now a climax in my life? Are there choices of direction now before me? (Pause) Perhaps. So I am to meet someone who can show me the way to Magical advancement. That would be wonderful, and most welcome. I wonder who it could be? It could be a person, even someone I already know. It could be a discarnate human being, even a non-human astral entity. Or perhaps, it is my Holy Guardian Angel, mine own Higher Self, my Oversoul, the I Am That I Am part of me, the everlasting Child of God Self. May it be so! (Pause. Stand.)

I am on Path Twenty-five. The twenty-fifth Path is the Administrative Intelligence, because it directs all the operations of the planets and concurs therein. To this path is assigned Sol, the Sun, the Hebrew letter Vau which means Nail, and Tarot XIX, the Sun. On the Noble Eightfold Path this is Right Rapture.
The Virtue is Rulership. The Sin is Pride. Let not this sin be mine. The Vice is Dictativeness. Let not this vice be mine.

Go deosil to south, put incense in Censer, cense Altar, go to west, face Altar, take Tarot Atu XIX, the Sun, hold it high and say:

Lord of the Fire of the World! Reveal to me your Mystery! (Lower card and gaze at it for a moment.) This card represents Solar Energy. We know that all the energy we have on earth comes to us from the Sun. The masters say, "In the Sun is the Secret of the Spirit." (Pause.) The secret of the spirit is—energy? The card depicts children—young human life—beginning of self-consciousness. The secret of the spirit is self-conscious energy! Spirit is Self-Conscious Energy! God is Spirit. God is Self-Conscious Energy!

Master Therion says that Atu XIX shows the Twins shining forth and playing. The twins are the Vau and final He of Tetragrammaton. Yod is Chokmah, the first He is Binah, Vau is Zoar Anpin which is Tiphareth with Chesed, Geburah, Netzach, Hod and Yesod as appendages, final He is Malkuth. Zoar Anpin is the Bridegroom. His bride is Malkuth, the Kingdom. The book 777 lists Atu XIX as representing the fighting of Horus and Set. Now Horus is Light, Set is Darkness. Here we have boy and girl, bridegroom and bride, light and darkness. This Path goes between the light and dark Pillars, the opposite principles. Opposite principles are such as male and female, light and dark, up and down, summer and winter, even good and evil. The fighting, the playing, of opposite principles. What does all this mean? (Replace card on Altar. Pause.)

Myriad are the pairs of opposites.
The opposing principles contend not.
Rather do they co-habit and co-operate
To produce the phenomena of the universe.
This is the Dual Manifestation of Truth.
Realization of it brings Right Rapture.

Pause in contemplation of what has just been said. Touch Kamea of the Sun.

> Sol, Great Sun! Seat and Symbol of the Cosmic Christ, the Cosmic Buddha! Thou Single Source of Light and Life whose scattered seeds we are on earth! Praise be unto thee! I hear your words—"Give forth thy light to all without doubt; the clouds and shadows are no matter for thee. Make Speech and Silence, Energy and Stillness twin forms of thy play." I hear and I obey.

Take the nail from Altar, stare at it for a moment, then say:

> The Hebrew letter Vau is assigned to this Twenty-fifth Path. Vau means nail. In Hebrew Vau is used as a connective, like we use the word "and". A nail is a fastener, it joins or binds. It connects things. Of course it is also a Dagger, a Sword, and a Rod, hence is masculine, positive, airy, fiery. Evidently it is of use to me in traversing this path. (Tuck nail under girdle.)

Go from west by north to east. Face eastern wall. Vividly visualize the Veil of Paroketh before you! Say:

> The Veil of Paroketh is before me. I cannot see beyond it. It hinders my further progress on this path. Beyond is Tiphareth, the Sphere of the Sun and the Seat of Christ-Consciousness, of Buddhic-Consciousness. But the glory of that is veiled to me. A Veil! The Veil of the Temple was rent at the time of the Crucifixion. Isis stands in the east, her beauty is veiled to the eyes of the profane. When a man looks upon her naked beauty he dies, for she takes him, he is joined to her, he is born anew, he becomes one with her. Christ suffers his Passion, nailed to a cross. "Unless a man die and be born again he can in no wise enter the Kingdom of Heaven." A rebirth is a transmutation. I aspire to Tiphareth Consciousness! When I attain that I will have attained Mastery. But the Veil of Paroketh presently bars me. I shall return to this place again! I shall return! Now let me explore the other Path.

Replace nail on Altar. Go deosil to north, face south. Say:

> I am now on Path Twenty-seven that leads from Hod to Netzach. The twenty-seventh Path is called the Renovating Intelligence because the Holy God renews by it all the changing things which are renewed by the creation of the worlds. To this path is assigned the Zodiacal Sign of Sagittarius, the Archer or the Centaur; the Hebrew letter Shin which means Tooth but represents Spirit, and Tarot Atu XIV, Temperance.

Go to Altar, take Tarot Atu XIV, hold it high and say:

> Daughter of the Reconcilers! Bringer Forth of New Life! Reveal to me your Mystery! (Lower card, gaze at it for a moment.) In your hands you hold two vases, emptying the contents of one into the the other. When you have done so you reverse the process, pouring back and forth, emptying each in turn into the other. Why do you do this? What does it mean? On your breast is a square, enclosing an upright equilateral triangle—the mystic Sign of the Taro. One of your feet is on dry land, the other in water. On your forehead is the symbol of the Sun. The glory of a golden Crown shines on a high mountain in the far distance behind you, a path leads thereto but

117

its course is lost in hilly terrain. Yellow iris blooms where you are standing. (Pause.) This is the Mystery of the Fourth Dimension, the Mystery of Time. We think of time as flowing in one direction only, from the past to the present to the future. This is so because the conscious mind is so structured as thus to perceive time. But in reality time flows in different directions and is not necessarily always linear in nature. (Pause.) In Tarot divination this card signifies promotion if dignified or upright and demotion if ill-dignified or upside down. Sagittarius is the Centaur, half animal, half human. The path shown in this card is the same path shown in the Waning Moon card, the path of evolution. Temperance, the Daughter of the Reconcilers, tells me evolution is not always necessarily forward, upward, for the better. The Centaur shows the animal transmuted by aspiration into the human. The Werewolf, on the other hand, shows the human transmuted by blood-lust into the animal. All this is associated with the Fourth Dimension. (Pause.) The Secret of this Path then is Transmutation.

Replace card on Altar. Touch Kamea of Jupiter and say:

Mighty Jupiter! Jove! Ruler of Sagittarius! All-Father in three forms of Fire, Air, Water! Generous giver of gifts! Greater benefic! The Magical Power I pray for is that of Transmutation. Base metal to gold, animal to human, human to divine! Hear my prayer addressed to thee, and as my will, so mote it be! I hear thy words— "Perfection presides over Transmutation. Self-sacrifice and self-control govern the wheel. Transmute all wholly into the images of thy will, bringing each to its true token of perfection." I hear, I seek to understand that I may obey.

Touch bow and arrow and say:

Diana! Huntress! Bringer Forth of Life! The Bow and Arrow are yours. They are assigned to this Rite. Go thou before me in the hunt.

Remove girdle, robe and sandals. Crouch, emulating the babe in the womb. Then be born as a primitive form of life, slithering along floor deosil around Altar. Then be a snake, a frog, a hoofed animal, an ape, hissing, croaking, grunting, making animal sounds, imitating animal movement. Several times around Altar. Then stand upright as a human, finish dance in the west. Reclothe. Say:

First the stone, then the plant, then the animal, then the human! I have transmuted from the animal to the human. I seek further transmutation.

Take the glass with brandy in right hand, the empty glass in left hand. Pour brandy from right to left, then reverse the process, saying:

Pour thine own freely from the vase in thy right hand, and lose no drop. Hath not thy left hand a vase?

Drink the brandy. Replace glasses. Take Cup and offer it, saying:

The Virtue of this Path is Directness. Direct may I ever be. (Offer Cup to the east.) I shall return! The Vice of this Path is Wastefulness. Wasteful may I never be. (Drink water in Cup. Replace Cup on Altar. Sit.) I see a rainbow stretching from Hod to Netzach! (Vividly visualize.) The Path of the Arrow goes straight up the Tree of Life

on the Middle Pillar of Mildness! The Bow of Promise is before me!
(Look to the east.) I shall return!

Enter the Silence. Perform Closing Exercises of Temple Rite.

COUNTER MAGIC TO BLACK MAGIC

The Theurgist who has performed most of the rites and ceremonies of this Book of Ritual Magic need have no fear of so-called magical "attacks" from practitioners of "Black Magic" since such performance will have given him an aura of such great magical strength as to be practically invulnerable. But just what is "Black Magic"? In the first place it is a misnomer, being a term used mostly by practitioners of one system of magic to refer to all other systems or schools not their own. This is especially true of those groups who do not think of their practices, rites and ceremonies as "magic". The Roman Catholic Mass, the Protestant Holy Communion, the Jewish Bar-Mitzvah, the Christian Science "treatment", baptism, confirmation, ordination, wedding and funeral ceremonies—the many rites of passage, of transformation, of initiation—of all religions, societies, cultures, are really magic practices. The New Thought Metaphysician thinking his "beautiful thoughts" and saying his "affirmations" is practicing magic along with the Buddhist or Catholic saying his Rosary and the Theurgist performing a Path Working. The Jewish housewife lighting candles just before sundown on Friday is practicing magic along with the priest or acolyte lighting candles in church for Vespers. "Followers of the Left Hand Path" are simply those who follow not the "Right Hand Path"—"right" here having the connotation of correct, genuine, real—in other words, "his" or "their" as opposed to "my" or "our" particular school of magical thought.

In the second place, "Black Magic" is a term used by many authorities and writers to refer to those magical practices which are malicious, vengeful or sadistic-masochistic in nature. Magic "power" being what it is—an amoral, neither moral nor immoral, a non- or supra-ethical etheric-astral energy, influenced, manipulated or controlled by conscious and sub-conscious mentations—it naturally follows that such energy can be put to use in whatever way the possessor chooses, either consciously or "driven" by those deeper and mostly unconscious "drives", "needs", or "urges", usually to be important, to have power or to gratify various hungers. Hence there are many levels of motivation in magic practice, ranging all the way from total dedication to the highest spiritual ideals to narrow-minded, perverse, "sick" self-centeredness. Those above an indeterminate, vague and wavering line of demarcation are called "white" or "good" magic, those below are termd "black" or "evil". Here, semantically speaking, we are co-relating "white" with "good" and "black" with "bad". This idea all Theurgists, both black-skinned and white-skinned, should find unacceptable. Even those groups and individuals who call themselves "Satanists" or "Devil Worshippers" are not necessarily dedicated to the popular concept of "evil", but rather to the practice and promulgation of a different approach to reality and a different set of life values.

The greatest magical power in the universe is, as everyone knows, love. Love is the Law, Love under Will. The ideal and the aim of the Theurgist should be to be so charged with the magical power of love that everyone and everything—friends and enemies, the kind and the envious, the generous and the malicious, ill and good wishes, curses and blessings, "good" and "evil"

119

spirits—that comes his way is bathed therein and affected thereby. Friends are blessed for being in his presence, enemies are transformed into friends, thought-forms are dissolved and their basic energy is transmuted, "good" spirits rejoice and "evil" spirits either flee or succumb to the "charm" of love and become "good".

We remember that "evil is unbalanced force, unbalanced force is evil." This ranges all the way from some degree of imbalance in practically every one of us, through the "Qlippothic Forces" which are the "shadows" or "the dark opposites" of the Sephirothic forces, to the great powers of Chaos. On the other hand, we also remember that "the opposing forces contend not, rather do they co-habit and cooperate to produce the phenomena of the universe"—the eternal play of Yin and Yang. Therefore we recognize that much of which we feel is "opposing" or "against" or "contrary to" us is in reality forces acting automatically in response to the stimulus of the primary action on our own part to accomplish something. If I attempt to throw a stone at a target, the inertia of the stone "opposes" the kinetic action of my muscles. If I do not exert enough energy, the stone falls short of the mark. If I exert too much, the stone overshoots the place intended. Therefore I must realize and calculate the inertia of the stone and take advantage of it so as to exert just the right amount of energy to hit the target. Even though the stone "opposes" the force of my arm, it is not really my enemy, it is just its own heavy self. In Magic, as in throwing a stone at a target, opposing forces must be accepted and so dealt with as to accomplish the purpose intended.

Nevertheless, until we attain the cosmic calm of the saint or great master or the "Ipsissimus" Magus, we need to keep our magical balance by being able to recognize and to know just how to deal with opposing magical forces.

The greatest counter magic to the so-called Black Magic practices is STRENGTH. Magical strength is attained by following the counsel of the old Magi to "invoke often." This means to keep "in shape" by regular and frequent magical "training" and "exercise." The tools of counter magic are knowledge of and experience in magic, a love and an understanding and a tolerance of and to all forms of life everywhere, and—a sense of humor!

The Evil Eye

"Overlooking" is the term used mostly by European witches for the practice of staring intently with eyes either narrowed or unusually wide open and head thrust forward while wishing bad luck or muttering a spell or curse such as, "Where you go, what you do, bad luck follow you!" or, "Lord of Mis-rule, follow, follow!" Of course, many envious people stare in malice at those whom they envy.

COUNTER MAGIC: Look the starer in the eye and say inaudibly, "The Lord within me greets the Lord within thee!", giving a friendly smile and a nod of the head. Seeing, accepting and transmuting the thought-form, "Hello, dirty green little maggot! Your energy is welcome, but you've got to change! Washerwoman, Washerwoman, cure the mange!" If you wish to show your contempt, give the Sign of the Old One and a hearty laugh or a superior little smile. If you're fearful of such glances (You must get over that!), wear a consecrated talisman such as the Kamea of Jupiter. Later, in all cases and to be certain, perform the Lesser Ritual of the Pentagram.

Magic Spells

An unusual streak of bad luck foreshadowed by premonitions of disaster and accompanied by feelings of hopelessness and doom is a sure sign that something is amiss in one's life. This may be the result of your own wrong attitude toward life or your own, perhaps temporary, wrong thought processes. After all, thoughts are things, and "as a man (or a woman, and especially a Theurgist!) thinketh in his heart, so is he." On the other hand, it also may be the result of some malicious magic! In either case, action is imperative.

First of all, ask these questions: Am I bringing all this bad luck on myself? If so, why? Could it be I am punishing myself for some real or imagined wrong-doing on my part? Be very honest with yourself in answering. Perhaps a consultation with a trusted advisor is called for. We all have mental and emotional blind-spots which we can't see but which the advisor perhaps can. At least a consultation with the Tarot, Rune Sticks or I Ching is indicated. Consider the possibility that you are punishing yourself for attempting to practice magic in the first place. This is not as amusing as it may first appear for many people, due to training in "orthodox" or "fundamentalist" religious background, have a sneaky feeling in the back of their minds that "all this magic stuff" is wrong, contrary to religious law, and therefore punishable. If this is so with you, then either give up your study of Magic and return back to the magic of your background religion or exorcise that idea once and for all. If for other reasons you realize your thinking processes have been amiss, then a reading of the books of Ernest Holmes or other popular metaphysicians would be helpful.

Finally, consider the possibility that some magician or witch is "binding" you or attempting to put a "spell" on you, either on their own initiative or at someone else's instigation, perhaps even being paid to do it. The basic motivations for this kind of magical attack are GREED, HATRED or LUST. Who would profit by your bad luck? Who hates you to the point of trying magically to do you harm? Who is lusting to have sexual relations with you, either the usual kind or perhaps the unusual? This latter type of magic practice is often indicated by sexual restlessness and dreams and the sensation that someone is attempting sexual play with you.

COUNTER MAGIC: A thorough cleansing of body and aura by a twenty-four hour fast taking only a little water, a long soaking ceremonial hot bath followed by a stinging cold shower, and finally the Greater Banishing Ritual of the Pentagram, banishing Earth, Air, Water and Fire in that order but **not** Spirit or Aether.

Curses

Most curses and cursing are nothing more than profanity expressed in fits of exasperation or anger. These create thought-forms that are evanescent, short-lived, whose energy is mostly expended in their creation. They should be disregarded or laughed off with love, understanding and perhaps sympathy for the exasperated or angry one.

In Magic, however, "curse" is the word for the heartfelt invoking and violent calling down of evil, misfortune, doom, upon another or others. It is also the word for the formula or charm intended to cause such misfortune.

To be magically effective a curse must be created and expressed (1.) under cataclysmic circumstances of enormous emotional stress by a person capable of almost cosmic hate and who is beside himself in a vast white-hot rage; (2.) coldly, carefully and deliberately by a person of great magical power which includes an almost superhuman will, a genius for the most intense concentration and an encyclopedic knowledge of occultism; or (3.) by a formal group of dedicated people, carefully prepared, performing ceremonially a precise and prescribed rite of malediction, imprecation or anathema. The curse may be upon (1.) a person, (2.) that person and certain others (such as first-born or male) or all of his family or descendents, (3.) a group of people who share something in common (such as guilt of an offense), or (4.) a place (such as a tomb, the curse to affect anyone who desecrates it). The curse may be general (such as bad luck or misfortune in general) or specific (violent death, early death, a particular illness or deformity, financial ruin, etc.). It may include or be accompanied or foreshadowed by psychic phenomena such as materialization of a form, often animal or monstrous in shape, or haunting of the thought-form or poltergeist variety, or teleportation of objects, or psychic winds or breezes, or odors, generally fetid. It may be timed to take effect on certain days or periods, or for a particular term, or whenever a specific situation arises (such as a tomb desecration). Finally, it may make use of an object-link with the person being cursed, or a power-object such as a talisman, a puppet, doll or statue, a parchment written in blood, a sword, etc.

COUNTER MAGIC: The above brief outline indicates the complexity of curses, and dealing magically with them is equally complex. The Theurgist should be well-experienced in magic before he attempts to combat a curse. In general, however, the procedure is (1.) if an object-link or power-object has been used, it is to be found, exorcised and destroyed (If one is suspected and not found, it may be visualized in the Cup and then exorcised.). (2.) A sacrifice or a gift is made (or restitution is done if any is called for and possible). (3.) A ceremonial cleansing is accomplished with fasting (one to three days) and bathing. And (4.) A banishing rite is performed (The most potent is the Greater Banishing Ritual of the Hexagram.).

The Pin-Stuck Doll

The picture in the popular mind of the toothless, stringy-haired old crone stooped over a low table in guttering candlelight viciously transfixing a doll with long pins is almost as standard an image of witchcraft as the equally caricatured beldame flying through the air on a broomstick. Both images are false and both are true but the first refers to a literal practice and the second to a highly symbolic act. False in the sense that whereas some witches may be old and unattractive, many are quite young and very attractive with the glistening smile of the white capped teeth of modern America. True in the sense that both pictures, even though caricatured, allude to valid magical practices. The broomstick riding witch signifies either the phenomena of astral projection or the practice of artificially stimulating sexual ecstacy so as to experience occult or psychic things. (The witch "rides" the broomstick by using it as a "dildo", or artificial penis, after "anointing" herself—vagina—and it with oil—lubricant—and so "flies" or "goes on a trip" of masturbatory fantasy to arrive at another state of consciousness in which communion with the "master", the "old one", takes place and the information or power asked for is received and a sense of "satisfaction" or "accomplishment" is attained.)

The pin-stuck doll is a puppet made usually of beeswax (nowadays, modeling clay) to represent the victim of the magical attack. An object-link is incorporated into or used as clothing for the puppet which is signed with and baptized in the name of the victim. The pin, or sometimes the dagger, is used to inflict a wound upon the puppet during a ceremony of intense concentration. The puppet is then hidden in the vicinity of the victim or buried where he will step over it. He is always given some inkling or hint or suggestion (usually in a roundabout way such as an anonymous letter with a crude picture of the impaled doll with his name on it) of the attack.

COUNTER MAGIC: The doll should be searched for, found, exorcised and destroyed with fire. If unfound, it may be visualized in the Cup and exorcised. If a note or anything which the puppet-maker has touched is available, then that is to be exorcised. It is a law of Magic that when a thought-form is created and sent to another and finds no point of entry in the other's aura it automatically returns to its place of origin. In other words, if the magic cannot "get to" the one for whom it is intended, it bounces back and works on the one who made it in the first place. This is why the wise Theurgist works no "black" magic. If the attack is on a friend or client of yours, cleanse his aura with the Greater Banishing Ritual of the Pentagram, then re-charge it with the Lesser (invoking) Ritual of the Pentagram.

Sending the Fetch

The broom-riding witch referred to above could be "sending forth her fetch", a quaint term applied to the projection of the astral body. Of course she could be out of the physical body on a mission of mercy or attending a coven or assemblage in the non-physical worlds. "Rising on the Planes" is the term often used in Magic for conscious travel in the Inner or Higher Realms of Consciousness and Being. If, on the other hand, she is on a mission of mischief, her "fetch" or astral body is working "black" magic in which case a clean aura is the best counter-magic for she then has no point of entry. On missions of either mercy or mischief, if someone on the physical level is to be contacted, etheric substance must accompany the astral body in order to make the contact as the etheric is the medium of exchange of energies between the astral and the chemical-physical. Since the etheric body is the "vital" or "energy" body, the astral-traveler is usually tired after such a mission and any hurts or wounds therein received affect the physical body also. In other words, the physical body in trance or sleep will manifest any wounds or hurts the astral-etheric receives even though the latter may be at a distance from its physical habitat. There is a large literature on Astral Projection which the Theurgist should become acquainted with. Begin with "The Projection of the Astral Body" by Sylvan Muldoon.

Incubus and Succubus

Incubi (male) and Succubi (female) were popular figures in medieval ecclesiastical demonology, being "imps" or "devils" who sought to besmirch the chastity of celibates by attempting to have (and many times succeeding in having) sexual intercourse with them. These creatures were, and are, thought-forms created by the minds of sexually frustrated people. Hence they are sexually attractive even if sometimes with exaggerated sex attributes such as huge breasts or enormous penises. And since the creating mind considers sexual activity to be religiously forbidden and "evil", the creatures are usually horned or tailed to signify that they are devils. During the heyday of monasticism many a night was spent in at first visualizing and "being tempted" by this fascinating yet loathsome would-be sex partner, then in "being overcome" by it to the point of orgasm, or valiantly fighting and overcoming it by fervent prayers and "thinking on other things", finally in the peaceful sleep of post-coital satisfaction, the troubled sleep of guilt or the exhausted but sweet sleep of battle won. The energy of a thought-form is expended when its purpose is fulfilled. Thus those thought-forms of sexual activity which succeeded caused no more trouble except when they in fulfilling themselves gave rise to other thought-forms of guilt. But the unsuccessful ones would return night after night, growing stronger by being fed with more unfulfilled desire and growing more fervent with the added strength. These creatures would then seek to fulfill their purpose by attacking other people in the vicinity. The others are always of the same sex as the creator of the thought-form but may be people who are too young or too old or sufficiently satisfied sexually or preoccupied with other matters or just not interested in having sexual relations with a "devil", a "wraith", an "imaginary being" or a "thought-form", whichever it is thought to be. Such attacks can be troublesome indeed, or at least irksome, causing fright, bewilderment, annoyance, nausea.

But the energy of a thought-form can be transmuted. Sex-energy can be sublimated to all kinds of constructive and useful activity. The very female young nun or the virile monk praying fervently to overcome the temptation of the devil was using a magically correct technique of transmutation. Even today in an age of greater sexual understanding and freedom incubi and succubi are still occasionally created and can sometimes be a nuisance. They can even be created deliberately (by masturbating and not reaching a climax) in intense and vivid visualization and then "projected" or sent (by effort of will and naming the "victim") to another person of the same sex as the masturbator-visualizer witch.

COUNTER MAGIC: The best counter magic to this kind of "attack" is a satisfying sex life for such allows not the thought-form to gain admittance into the aura. Prayer and "thinking of other things" absorbs the energy and transmutes it. The Lesser Ritual of the Pentagram is most effective.

AFTERWORD

Much remains to be done. The "Watchtowers" or Elemental Tablets and Tablet of Spirit, the Tattwas and the Tattvic Tides, the Path Workings above the Veil of Paroketh, "Rising on the Planes", the Lotus Wand, the Magic Ring, the "Vault of the Adepti" are among those magic practices yet to be considered. But enough has been given in this book for the student to lay a firm foundation in practical Ritual Magic.

Most students of the occult long to be initiated into the Mysteries. They yearn for "One Who Knows" to show them "the Way." They envision a Fraternity of Adepts and Masters and fervently hope to become a member thereof. They join various occult organizations and by correspondence or in person are "initiated." Many such organizations are valid, having true links with the Elder Brothers of Mankind. Others vary from a group of sincere students seeking to work together in occult studies and practice, to groups surrounding and following a particular teacher or guru who may be truly an Initiate or Adept or may be an imposter or a fanatic with a system of teachings borrowed from others or originated by himself, to commercial enterprises selling "occult secrets and methods" which are easily obtainable from any fair-sized public library. Difficult indeed it is to learn the first Virtue of the Path—that of Discrimination. Our advice is to either "join 'em all" or "join 'em none" according to the personal proclivity of the seeker and to experience either the great joy or the deep disillusionment in full stride, accepting either as an initiatory experience, an expansion of consciousness.

It takes a Master Mason to "raise" the candidate to the position of a Master Mason. Baptism can be conferred only by a baptized person. So in Theurgy there is the belief that only a more advanced occultist can bestow magic powers upon a beginner. But the "more advanced" need not necessarily be a physical man, indeed may well be the "Higher Self" of the Seeker. After all, Life itself is the Great Initiator, the Cosmos of Many Mansions is the Great Graded Lodge Hall and the Holy Guardian Angel is the Hierophant who introduces us to the Mysteries. And we have the promise that when the pupil is ready the teacher will appear. So mote it be.

Blessed be!